Architecture
in
Philadelphia:
A Guide

The MIT Press
Cambridge,
Massachusetts,
and
London,
England

Architecture in Philadelphia: A Guide

Edward Teitelman

Richard W. Longstreth

Special Consultant,
George E. Thomas

Copyright © 1974 by
The Massachusetts Institute of Technology

This book was designed and produced by
The MIT Press Media Department.

It was set in IBM Composer Univers,
printed on Mead Moistrite Matte
by Halliday Lithograph Corporation,
and bound in G.S.B. S/535/83
by Wm. F. Zahrndt & Son Inc.
in the United States of America.

Library of Congress Cataloging
in Publication Data

Teitelman, Edward.
  Architecture in Philadelphia.

  Bibliography: p.
  1. Architecture—Philadelphia. I. Longstreth,
Richard W., joint author. II. Title.
NA735.P5T44   917.48'11'044   74-6070
ISBN 0-262-20028-7

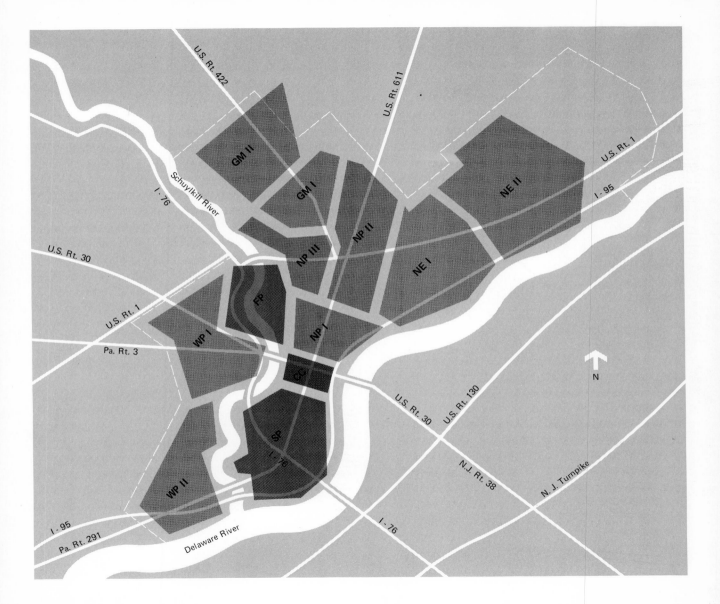

Contents

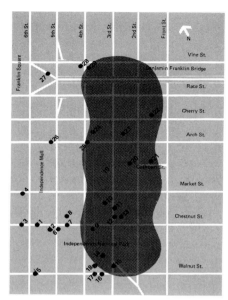

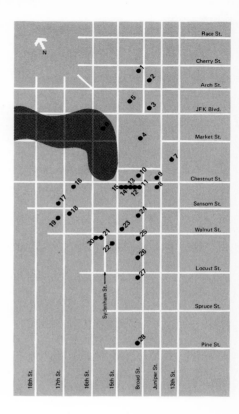

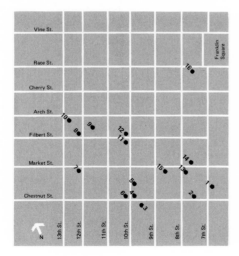

CC VI
90

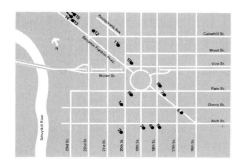

Fairmount Park
114

FP
116

CC VII
106

North Philadelphia
128

NP I
130

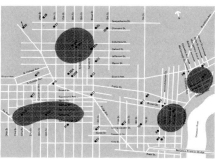

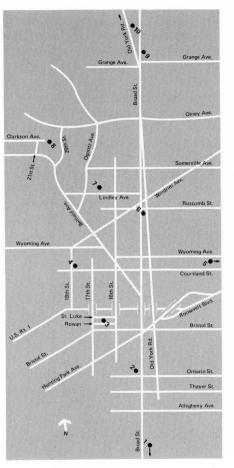

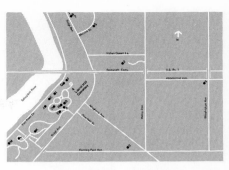

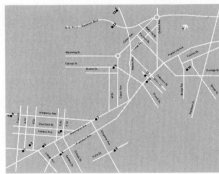

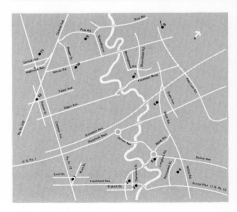

South Philadelphia
172

SP
174

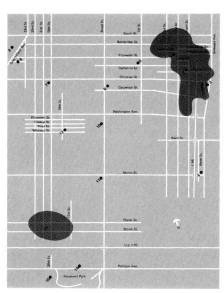

West Philadelphia
182

WP I
184

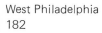

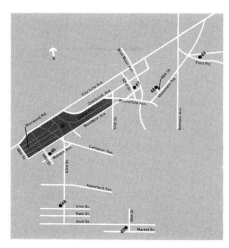

WP I
185

WP II
208

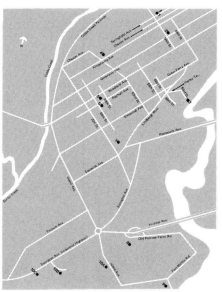

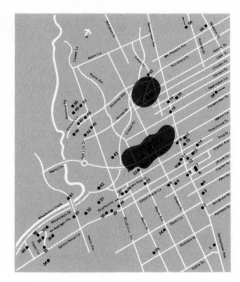
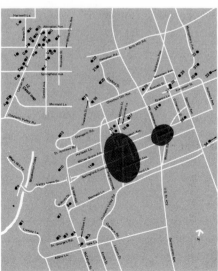

Notes to the Reader

Structures have been selected on the basis of architectural, planning, or city-scape value, and no legal responsibility is assumed either for the competency or accuracy of any of the listings included herein or for the appreciation or depreciation in value of any premises listed by reason of their inclusion. The fact that a building is listed does not indicate the owner's or occupant's permission to trespass, invade privacy, or destroy property, and permission should be obtained prior to visiting any privately owned dwelling. Almost all structures bear the original, earliest known, or most architecturally important owner's name or designation, and this does not necessarily represent their current occupant. Although we have attempted to note major changes in identity, some confusion may result, especially downtown, if the visitor asks for a structure by name rather than by address.

· Due to space limitations and considerations of emphasis, architects involved primarily with exterior and/or interior renovations or restorations have not been noted, except in instances where it is felt that their significance warrants inclusion. For convenience, we have attempted to date buildings from the onset of construction except where periods of design and construction have exceeded three years. As frequently as possible, architectural firm names are given as they were officially listed as of the date of construction. The geographical location of firms situated outside the area covered by this book is noted at the first citation in the text. Assignment of architects, dates, and owners reflects our judgments from the latest research available to us when the manuscript was prepared for publication (fall 1971, updated February 1973). Where there is any significant question, approximate dates and/or attributions have been specifically marked. It is hoped that as further research is conducted, the authors might be informed of new material and corrections to the published text so that future revisions might be as accurate and comprehensive as possible.

The maps in this book, by their nature, are limited in their coverage, frequently omitting less important streets. Not drawn to scale, they are intended to assist in the precise location of buildings. While these abstracts in many cases will suffice, an area map can prove a useful supplement.

The listings in downtown Philadelphia are grouped for touring by foot but not as formal walking tours. The narrow streets, limited parking, trolley cars, and heavy traffic make automobile use too frustrating, save on Sunday morning. Center City public transit is excellent and may be counted upon when feet give out.

Listings in the book are grouped by location, in smaller groups within general area designations that form the major divisions of the work. These major areas have general significance and correspond roughly to divisions of the city commonly used. The subgroupings, however, were developed largely to create manageable units for consideration and are arbitrary. Each entry is numbered to indicate the area and subgroup by a letter abbreviation of the area name and a Roman numeral for the subgroup (for example, CC I 4, NP II 20). The abbreviations are as follows: Center City-CC; Fairmount Park-FP; North Philadelphia-NP; The Northeast-NE; South Philadelphia-Sp; West Philadelphia-WP; Germantown-GM. The entries follow a general form: listing number, building name(s); date(s) and architect(s) of construction or modification, location, and comments.

As the book was originally developed as a part of a larger regional guide, a small number of structures within the city limits (mainly located in the far Northeast and Northwest) have not been included as they are better considered in a group with adjoining suburban development. Likewise several suburban structures appear here, in what are relatively cohesive groups.

Acknowledgments

This book is the result of a number of years of research by the authors as well as extensive work pooled from the investigations and studies of many scholars of the region. The financial assistance of the American Philosophical Society to Dr. Teitelman, through three grants from the Penrose and Johnson Funds, is acknowledged with sincere appreciation as is earlier support by the Philadelphia Historical Commission.

Beyond the usual gratitude to our wives and families for their toleration of seemingly endless years of preoccupation, and their general support, the authors especially wish to thank Mildred O. Teitelman, who devoted many hours and much work directly toward the production of this book. Mildred Osinski, who typed the final manuscript as a familial contribution, did much to make preparation of this book feasible.

The encouragement and active help of James O'Gorman, W. Robertson Paton, George Tatum, and Margaret Tinkcom have been invaluable in advancing our basic research and building listings to the point that a publishable effort could be considered and have continued through all stages of the work.

Among the many individuals who have been of assistance we thank especially: Alfred Branam, Jr., John Cooledge, Nathalie Davis, Marion Davis, Mrs. Kenneth Day, Robert Ennis, Jonathan Fairbanks, James Foss, David Gebhard, Irving Glazer, Constance Grief, John Harbeson, Beth Lattimore, Miriam Lesley, John Maass, James Massey, Moira Mathieson, Roger Moss, Peter Mooz, Hyman Myers, J. Ramsey Pennypacker, Carolyn Pitts, John Poppeliers, Hannah Roach, Morris Rosenthal, James Van Trump, Richard Webster, and Charles Woodward.

In addition the following architects and architectural firms have been extremely helpful in providing the authors with both information on their own work and historical material: The Ballinger Company (Louis deMoll); Edward H. Bernstein; Bower & Fradley; Armand Carroll; Carroll, Grisdale & Van Alen; Cope & Lippincott (Mather Lippincott); Demchick, Berger & Dash; Garner & White; Geddes, Brecher, Qualls & Cunningham; Paul Henon Associates; Louis I. Kahn; Vincent G. Kling & Associates; Kneedler, Mirick, Zantzinger,

Pearson, Ilvonen, Batcheler; Joel Levinson; Thaddeus Longstreth; Magaziner & DiGiorgio; Louis McAllister; Mitchell & Giurgola; Montgomery Bishop & Arnold; MurphyLevyWurman; Richard & Dion Neutra Associates; Charles Okie; Norman Rice; Louis Sauer; Frank Schlesinger; Harry Sternfeld; Stonorov & Haws; Walter Thaete; William Heyl Thompson; James Reid Thomson; Horace Trumbauer; Venturi & Rauch; Vollmer-Knowles; Wallace, McHarg, Roberts & Todd; and Frank Weise.

Access to the preliminary research efforts of the following students in the Graduate School of Fine Arts, University of Pennsylvania, is acknowledged: Carol Eaton (Willis Hale); Richard Derman (John Fraser); Elizabeth Langhorne (Addison Hutton); Theodore Sande (Theophilus Chandler); Linda Henefield Skalet (Wilson Eyre).
We are especially indebted to the staffs of the Philadelphia Historical Commission, the Historical Society of Pennsylvania, the Historic American Buildings Survey of the National Park Service, the Free Library of Philadelphia, and the University of Pennsylvania Fine Arts Library. The Avery Architectural Library of Columbia University, the Henry Francis du Pont Winterthur Museum Libraries, and the Library of the University of Delaware have also been most helpful. We also acknowledge with thanks the assistance of the following Historical Societies: Chestnut Hill Historical Society, Germantown Historical Society, and West Philadelphia Historical Society.

Photography Credits

All photographs in this book were taken by the authors (principally R.W.L.) or are from their collections, with the following exceptions: CC VIII 7, Rollin R. LaFrance; NE II 10, George Thomas; WP II 8, Jack Boucher (Historic American Buildings Survey); GM I 44 and GM I 46, original photographs from the Philadelphia Chapter/AIA Yearbooks, used with the Chapter's permission.

A Brief Historical Review of Architecture and Planning in Philadelphia

While still in London in 1681, William Penn developed an idealistic conception for a utopian settlement of considerable size to be placed in his newly won proprietory province in the New World. As an initial step to raise the necessary money he planned to sell 100 shares, each representing 5000 acres of country land. Two percent of this property would be in the "Greene Country Towne," or "Liberties," laid out in such a manner that in its original conception it would have had to extend in a mile-wide strip fifteen miles along the Delaware River. Here, in the "great town," the settlers would build their principal homes, each having access to navigable water. Central to the Liberties, at a convenient harbor, was to be a small commercial settlement with its area (set at 200 acres) apportioned to owners and renters of larger tracts.

But the settlement of the Delaware Valley had begun over forty years previously with the founding of a Swedish trading post at Fort Christina (now Wilmington) in 1638. Five years later Governor Johan Printz established a post farther up the Delaware at Tinicum,

just below the southwest border of present-day Philadelphia. Other concentrations of settlers began to form at Upland (now Chester) and Kingsessing, and, although Swedish rule ended in 1655, the people remained and continued to thrive, extending over a fair portion of the region. By the late 1670s English Quakers had also begun moving into the area, principally on the eastern side of the Delaware River, where they established the town of Burlington (New Jersey) in 1677.

Upon this primitive but surprisingly well settled area, Penn had intended to apply the grand conception of his Holy Experiment. But the original plans clearly could not fit. When his emissaries arrived to lay out Philadelphia around the nucleus of the port at Upland, they discovered that most of the land they would need was already occupied, and they eventually settled on the current location. Centered around the small cove at what became known as Dock Creek, the land was held by several owners willing to sell and had large adjoining unsettled acreage inland where the Liberties could be placed. Facing what was regarded as a hostile environment, the participants in the venture pressed for a more urban development than Penn had planned. Following Penn's arrival in late autumn of 1682 and a series of compromises and quick improvisations, the settlement began. Those who were ready to build received land along the Delaware, so that the city might assume an established appearance; investors who did not settle were given lots on land Penn bought along the Schuylkill. Construction was energetically pursued to the point that when Penn returned to London in 1684 he reported that some 357 houses had already been erected.

The 1682 plan of the city appears to have been closely patterned after Richard Newcourt's 1666 proposal for the rebuilding of London after the Great Fire of the same year, the chief elements of which—a grand central square at the intersection of axial streets (to be called "High" and "Broad"), symmetrically placed subordinate squares, and a grid pattern of streets—were taken up in the proposal for Philadelphia by Penn's surveyor, Thomas Holme. If not especially original (it also had similarities to nearby Burlington) or the first planned city in the country (for example, New Haven in 1638 and Charleston ca. 1670), it was of a size (two square miles) and scope that made it unique in the English colonies.

Although rather conservative compared with contemporary English and French Baroque schemes, more than any other community on the eastern seaboard it was a reflection of the ideals of the Age of Reason. Even with the further compromises that were to follow, Philadelphia's sense of order and established matrix of growth contrasted significantly with other communities' random collection of narrow, angled streets haphazardly placed. Part of the compromise had involved enlargement of the city, making it, rather than the Liberties, the principal settlement. Still Holme's plan, while distinctly urban in its system, attempted to retain the character of the country town Penn considered so important, with free-standing houses set on ample lots, gardens and yards surrounding each. But even this remnant soon succumbed to economic and social pressures. An increasing number of small, narrow houses were erected adjoining each other along the streets, and before 1700 the generous blocks themselves were subdivided by alleys where smaller houses were often built.

The buildings of the Swedes consisted of simple one- and two-room structures constructed from stones and logs. The log cabin was introduced to the New World here by them. While it has achieved a certain legendary status, after initial settlement it did not remain prominent in this region, and only a very few examples of these early log buildings survive (for example, in Delaware County). The Swedes' churches are a cultural legacy, but as all extant were erected after 1698, they represent an almost complete assimilation of English principles of design (see SP I 3).

The English initially also built wooden structures often following the Swedish model. However, the soil proved to be excellent for brickmaking, and eventually this form of masonry construction became the dominant building method. The early buildings were unsurprisingly small and simple in adornment. Aside from their somewhat awkward proportions, with steep roofs, and such variant details as diamond-paned windows and clustered chimneys, the general character of these houses was far more Renaissance than medieval. As such they were considerably more advanced than most urban dwellings erected elsewhere at that time, possibly reflecting the emigration from London of a number of carpenters no longer employed in the rebuilding after the Great Fire. The majority of the rural buildings were far less advanced, dwellings acting more as a fortress from the elements than as a focus for the cultivation of them (for example, the William Brinton House, 1704, near Dilworthtown). The notable exception was Penn's own country place in Bucks County, "Pennsbury" (1692), which was, if the reconstruction bears any similarities in character to the original, unquestionably one of the most splendid houses in the Colonies. Laid out in a manner more like later Georgian plantations in Virginia and South Carolina, it establishes a sense of order and dominance over the terrain in a manner suggestive of Penn's attitude toward planning and, indeed, his philosophy of civilization itself.

The Georgian Period

By the 1720s Philadelphia was emerging as one of the Colonies' most substantial urban areas and was clearly the most sophisticated. As much a center of commerce as of science and the arts, the city had grown by mid-century to be the second largest in the British Empire. The values of the divergent and often conflicting elements, which are responsible for any metropolitan growth, began to coalesce into two major and distinct, if interrelated, architectural attitudes. On the one hand, there was a splendid ornate Georgian, inevitably reminiscent of London and frequently more sumptuous in its details than could be found elsewhere in the colonies. On the other hand, there was the conservative and studied austerity of the buildings of the Quakers. Christ Church (see CC I 20) (begun 1727) and the Greater Meeting House (1755), which once stood a block to the south, illustrate the differences at an extreme.

In form as well as detail, the Georgian buildings in the city were among the most sophisticated to be found along the Eastern Seaboard. So venturesome a structure as the State House (see CC I 1) (begun ca. 1730) was then unique as a civic expression, but visually not an isolated anomaly. Domestic architecture in scale and interior embellishment was often of similar pretension; while much of it has disappeared, the Neave and Abercrombie Houses (after 1758) (CC II 7 and 8) and the Powel House (1765) (see CC II 3) give some indication of the magnificence achieved.

It is interesting that no one figure comparable with William Buckland or Peter Harrison appears to have been responsible for the major local eighteenth-century structures. This could, in part, be due to the guildlike Carpenters' Company, which apparently controlled virtually all building that was conducted in the city. Robert Smith in his ecclesiastical work is the only master builder who attained a significant reputation. Gentlemen amateurs sketched out a few edifices such as the State House, but the carpenter still determined the final form of the building.

Juxtaposed with the individual architectural monuments was an equally distinct sameness fostered by the simplicity of the Quaker architecture, in keeping both with their religious philosophy and the building traditions they had known in England. Somewhat varied, house-by-house, but with a prevailing unity of basic materials and small scale, Philadelphia had many aspects of a straightened-out, intensified, block-on-block Buckinghamshire village. The unvarying lines of the streets, with the regularity of their intersections, helped secure an impression of the routine, subduing individual variations in facades and giving rise to a reputation of monotony. The most indicative Quaker buildings have been the meetinghouses. Most are astute studies in sensitivity to material and proportion, and although elements reflect the periods of their construction, they possess a certain timelessness in their expression of the abstract.

The Liberties laid out inland to the north of the city were only sparsely settled, but the banks of both the Schuylkill and Delaware Rivers continued to attract development. Through the eighteenth century a number of great houses were erected there, often as elaborate as civic and ecclesiastical design in the city. While all traces of these have long since disappeared along the Delaware, Fairmount Park has preserved many that were built along the Schuylkill. Farther into the country these formal structures were the exception. Rural areas began to develop an important indigenous architecture essentially Quaker in character, the finest results of which appeared in the stone farmhouses that have characterized the region and have provided a continued influence on its architecture. Basically Georgian, these houses were often built over a period of years, being added to as the owners acquired the means or developed the need for additional space. The result was a spontaneous and completely natural mass, often asymmetrical, responding to basic needs but revealing a strong and subtle sensitivity to form and the general character of the land.

When tastes in architecture began to shift, after the Revolution, and to coalesce, after the establishment of the national government, into a Federal style, builders in Philadelphia remained content to erect Georgian designs with only slight variation. Nevertheless, there were some notable exceptions that were comparable with the finest work of the period in New England or the South.

The President's House (1792-1797) was ruefully demolished not many years after it was completed but represented one of the grandest endeavors in the country at the time. The Center Pavilion of the Pennsylvania Hospital (1794-1805), designed by David Evans the Younger, is another principal monument of the style (see CC III 11). Both Dr. William Thornton, before he won the National Capitol competition, and Major Pierre Charles L'Enfant left their mark on the city; Samuel Blodgett's First Bank of the United States (1797) was one of the most impressive heralds of the change (CC I 14). The First Bank appears in the background of photograph CC I 15.

Still, the members of the Carpenters' Company remained the main force in building. In an era of considerable expansion, when the city began to spill out to the north of its intended boundary, most of the new structures were little more than variations on what had already occurred. The Carpenters' Company 1786 Rule Book and even Owen Biddle's Young Carpenter's Assistant published in 1805, which were used as the standard models for building, gave little indication of the very radical shifts in style that were occurring elsewhere. Many structures of this period (such as the bulk of what exists today in Society Hill) (CC II) bear close similarity to their predecessors of a number of years.

This is probably a reflection of the conservative nature of the populace. But more important was the fact that Philadelphia had achieved her considerable stature before the Revolution; her institutions had undergone their initial period of development and were now primarily concerned with consolidation rather than innovation. Most other cities were really only beginning to establish comparable status for themselves and were predictably more receptive to new architectural concepts that could be associated with their new prosperity.

The changes that did occur in Philadelphia did so very slowly. Gradually through the first decades of the nineteenth century houses grew in scale and size, generally becoming simpler in detail and more austere in appearance. Variants of this sort of dwelling continued to be standard through to the 1850s when the Brownstone came into vogue. It was in the early 1800s that the house row grew to a prevalent status. An obviously profitable solution for the land speculator, the number of these often very fine blocks quickly increased until they dominated the residential areas of the city. Even most nonrow dwelling construction occurred as semidetached or twin houses until the latter part of the century, and the row house has continued to be a standard form in the city to the present day.

Architects and Classical Forms

It was Philadelphia's prominence that attracted Benjamin Henry Latrobe from Virginia in 1798. A brilliant, sensitive architect and engineer, far advanced for his time, he had been professionally trained in his native England and arrived in this country as the first man to bear that distinction. While he entered a society that was often unsympathetic to his creativity (as architects' services were still generally regarded as an unnecessary luxury and the unpredictability of scientific experimentation in engineering was not always tolerated), he nevertheless made a very significant impression upon the city's architectural development and presented the first serious challenge to either the amateur designers or the seemingly impregnable position of the Carpenters' Company.

Stylistically, his designs represented what was felt to be a return to antique prototypes, which in many respects closely conformed to English Neo-Classical examples of the period. But aside from both this and the important nationalistic connotations that his revived Greek forms were quickly to assume, Latrobe's Philadelphia work marked a fundamental shift in architectural expression in this country, emphasizing mass and the use of geometric form in buildings consciously conceived in abstract terms. The end result still retained a certain Federal scale and delicacy, and while more antique elements were often incorporated, they were still freely adapted to serve contemporary building functions.

Taught by both Latrobe and Thomas Jefferson, Robert Mills was inheritor of much of their flair for innovation as well as Latrobe's highly professional attitude toward his work. The style of his designs remained very much under the influence of Latrobe while he was in Philadelphia, experimenting freely with classical forms but with a sound knowledge of precedent. It was not until he left the city that his works began to assume a strong personal character.

Both architects stayed in the city only a few years, designing a relatively small number of buildings, almost all of which have long since been demolished. A talented but hardly original amateur such as John Dorsey borrowed directly from them and received far more commissions by virtue of the fact that he worked for little or no fee. Still Latrobe and Mills had enormous influence on the ensuing decades. Partly as a result of their example, the concept of the architect was beginning to change in the public's mind, and through their work Philadelphia assumed a position of principal leadership in the development of the Greek Revival in America.

It was William Strickland, as much as any other architect, who was responsible for bringing the style to its prominence in the city. Achieving distinction with his winning design for the Second Bank of the United States (1818-1824, see CC I 7) his work embodied a creative archaeological approach that extended the Greek Revival to a high level of sophistication and freed it of its Federal vestiges. With some of the subtleties of Greek monumentality, sympathetically reinterpreted to the Philadelphia streetscape, his best buildings became dominant focuses in the city, achieving, through different means, what the Georgian churches and State House complex had done over half a century earlier. Strickland appears to have had more of an interest in the refinement of his achievement than in further experimentation. His approach met with considerable success, and he was able to conduct a flourishing practice for some thirty years, designing many of the city's more important buildings. In addition, his seldom discussed planning efforts have an unobtrusive dignity that fits well into the pattern of the city. Unfortunately such farsighted projects as the plan for Cairo, Illinois (1838), or a scheme for the redevelopment of virtually the entire Philadelphia waterfront for Stephen Girard (1836) never materialized.

Of no less importance was John Haviland whose austere, brutal interpretation of forms was the opposite in approach to that of Strickland. His designs show his interest in expressing a strong abstraction of form, with archaeological style seemingly of secondary importance. While parallels can be seen with Latrobe's work, both in attitude and scale, Haviland gave considerably more emphasis to pure geometric expression, and even in his more academic Classical designs the simple massiveness rests in contrast to Latrobe's delicate balance between solids and voids.

All of the early architects to some degree also engaged in the more exotic Gothic, Egyptian, and Chinese modes. Latrobe's awkward and naïve Sedgeley (1799) was one of the earliest endeavors in the country in a style best called Gothick (to separate it from the later Gothic Revival) (FP I 4). Mills and Strickland made similar infrequent indulgences in the picturesque. Haviland was particularly known for his Gothic and Egyptian Revival prisons. Although their later works became more archaeologically credible, these styles were nonetheless still employed more for their literary significance and associative connotations; most of the buildings were essentially classical in their predominant attitude of order and symmetry.

The other primary form giver of the Classical Revival in Philadelphia was Thomas Ustick Walter, whose work was often as florid as Haviland's was stark. In this light, it is interesting that his efforts were perhaps the most successful in achieving monumentality in large commissions. Certainly his adroitness in manipulating classical forms on a very large scale is evidenced by Founder's Hall for Girard College (1833-1847) (see NP I 18). Haviland's work, while far more massive in appearance, lacked a sensitivity to scale and when executed in too large a size tended to sacrifice monumentality for oppressiveness; Strickland's more subdued assertions became unconvincing once they exceeded certain dimensions. These were falterings in the style which were not uncommon either for architects or builders in the country. Walter was one of the very few men of his era who could have enjoyed in the additions to the United States Capitol (1851-1865) the same degree of success he had attained in his smaller buildings. The Capitol became probably the first building in the nation which could rival the great palaces of Europe in civic grandeur if not in refinement. On the other hand, several buildings he executed in the small town of West Chester, Pennsylvania, are almost equally monumental but rendered in a scale entirely sensitive to the size and nature of the community.

Although principally known for his later work in New York, Napoleon LeBrun played an important role in Philadelphia as well. A student of Walter's, he designed works difficult to classify within the framework of then contemporary American architecture. His two major commissions here, the Cathedral of Saints Peter and Paul (1846-1864) (CC VII 8) and the American Academy of Music (1855) (see CC V 27), as conceived, were closely derived from the Neo-Baroque that was then becoming popular in France. Their grandiose, heavily embellished spaces were a somewhat abrupt departure from Philadelphia's past. Lesser works, however, were usually executed with more conventional means.

Trends to the Romantic

Evolving concurrently with the mature Classical Revival was the Romantic movement, a principal member of which was John Notman. Although the extent of his work has yet to be fully evaluated and his buildings are not widely known outside the area, it is certain that he played a very significant part in the development of early Victorian architecture in America. Having emigrated from Scotland in 1831, he had a firsthand knowledge of current British design. In part inspired by the works of John Nash, he erected what is credited as being the first Italianate villa in the country for Bishop Doane (1837), which stood until recently in Burlington, New Jersey. A beautiful and sophisticated study in asymmetrical balance, it received immediate attention through illustration in Andrew Jackson Downing's widely circulated books and exerted enormous influence on ensuing country house design. The style was, in turn, applied to urban commissions, but now with an emphasis on the symmetrical rectilinearity of the Italian Renaissance. With such works as the Athenaeum (1845) (see CC III 1), Notman did much to foster the formal and urbane approach that was to gain immense popularity during the next three decades. Indeed he may well have designed the first house in the country faced in the brownstone with which the style is so commonly associated. Along with Richard Upjohn of New York, his ecclesiastical work in the vocabulary of the English rural Gothic was instrumental in bringing a maturation and relevance to the American Gothic Revival.

Of no less importance to the Romantics was landscape design. Notman's Laurel Hill Cemetery (NP III 4) exemplified the adaptation of wild acreage for its own sake as well as the picturesque juxtaposition of man-made objects in nature. The same approach was applied by the engineers and planners of the rapidly developing Fairmount Park, which grew along the Schuylkill River from a nucleus at the Waterworks (see FP I 1). Incorporating a balance of winding roadways, wild glens, and open pastures with a restrained number of visual landmarks (including Georgian houses and Centennial buildings), it represents planned Romantic naturalness at its very best. It also set the notable precedent of keeping the river free from exploitation, protection that in later years was extended to include creek valleys elsewhere in the city.

Samuel Sloan was the most prolific contributor to the Romantic ethic in Philadelphia. While possibly not possessing the same degree of originality as Notman, he executed a wide variety of commissions including great Gothic, Italianate, and Moorish villas. He was responsible for some of the most sumptuous town houses erected in the city as well as numerous speculative ventures, particularly in then suburban West Philadelphia. But he is probably best known for his institutional work, which seems to have represented a continuation of the Quaker tradition of simple, functional building. Many of his schools and hospitals set standards for organization and design that had wide following in this country and abroad.

A separate commercial architecture as such evolved in the early nineteenth century, and the work in Philadelphia after 1820 is considered to be as important as that of New York or Boston in the development of later functional architecture. Resulting from a period of flourishing trade, these mainly anonymous structures once comprised a large and cohesive district along the Delaware River. The Independence National Park in the 1950s destroyed a majority of the most significant examples, not the least of which, the Jayne Building by William L. Johnston and Thomas U. Walter (1849), was generally regarded as the country's first protoskyscraper. The remnants of the district to the north of the Park remain—threatened (see CC I 19).

Joseph Hoxie and Stephen Button were two designers of commercial buildings who achieved a clarity of architectonics without violating the sense of structure or denying the building's intended use that was quite exceptional for the time. Unfortunately the majority of their numerous noncommercial commissions were mediocre, their clumsy handling of Italianate forms often providing unintended comic relief.

The effects of the Civil War were of sufficient magnitude to relegate the Romantic ethic in architecture to a subordinate position, with almost all the optimistic, straightforward, and slightly naïve aspects of its approach becoming greatly subdued in a materialistic and pretentious mixing of styles. The years that followed saw the continued spread of urban development into areas adjoining the old city (the city annexed the rest of the county in 1854). But with few exceptions, the prominent architects of the prewar era had little influence in this expansion. Variants of the so-called Second Empire Style never gained the immense popularity in Philadelphia that they did elsewhere throughout the country. Nonetheless, one of the most significant achievements of the movement is City Hall (see CC V 4), which attains the symbolic (civic) monumentality so eagerly sought after in this "national" style. Its creator, John McArthur, Jr., was a competent but hardly exceptional architect, and, in comparison to the bulk of his work, City Hall is especially remarkable. As with the Second Empire, the High Victorian Gothic and the later Romanesque Revival also were never prevalent.

A large portion of the buildings erected
in the 1870s and 1880s were strongly
regional in character, although identifiable with construction of the era elsewhere. To some extent this was due to
Frank Furness, who in 1866 established
practice in Philadelphia after training in
the then radical office of Richard Morris
Hunt in New York. A brilliant designer
of practical and stylishly upsetting structures, he became the city's preeminent
architect for nearly two decades. With
the force of his personality and the
dearth of comparable talent in Philadelphia at that time, the influence of his
work appears to have been very strong
throughout the city and its surrounding
area.

In Furness's youthful work, much of
which was his finest, Hunt's sophistication and experimentation were reflected
along with the influence of such European contemporaries as Ruskin and
Viollet-le-Duc. A keen admiration for
the strong mercantile tradition in the
city was also seen combined with his
own maniacal love for contradiction.
That he was one of the earliest American architects actively to pursue the use
of negative elements as a vocabulary of
architectonic expression is an aspect
that renders Furness particularly significant. It was in part an expression of his
rebellion against the austere Quaker
simplicity that was still so dominant in

existing buildings throughout the city.
His considerably better known contemporary, H. H. Richardson, justly received
recognition for the order and clarity he
brought to design; Furness's work, on
the other hand, emphasized the heterogeneous and uncertain state of the period with a haunting deliberateness that
could border on parody. Unlike his less-
ers who heaped a more or less standard
bonanza of conceits on what were basically simple structures, Furness would
construct a fundamentally complex
structure and express it in a clear, if
awkward and often insulting, manner. In
the old library at the University of
Pennsylvania (1888-1891) (see WP I 13)
he developed a series of flagrant Pirane-
sian spaces, enjoying the discomfort of
direct confrontation of masonry and
iron construction. Where vast expanses
of raw steel "atrociously" join frantic
piles of masonry, fig leaves mockingly
cover the "meeting place."

On the other hand, a sense of rational
order and clarity, certainly related to
the Quaker precedent, became increasingly important in Furness's later work.
While occurring partly as the result of
personal maturation and changes in the
cultural climate, as well as the ascen-
dency of Allen Evans as a design partner
in the firm, there was evidence of this
strain in the early years of his practice,
as indicated in his long-demolished
Jefferson Medical College Hospital of

1875. The austere, simple houses standing at 2206-2208 Walnut Street (probably ca. 1873) again contrast sharply with the once-adjoining Livingston House (1887), which represents the more popular conception of Furness's work. More sizable buildings in later years, such as the Merion Cricket Club (1895) and the demolished Broad Street Station (1893), employed a heavy terra-cotta masonry interaction, reiterated in the forms themselves, which created a direct if somewhat weak expression.

If the qualities that distinguish Furness above his eccentricity were not entirely shared by his contemporaries, there nonetheless was a certain similarity in attitude, but as is frequently the case such a bond was not necessarily apparent at the time. There is a prevailing awkward ugliness in Philadelphia design of the period which it is difficult to believe was wholly unintentional. The brooding and inherently gloomy atmosphere is perhaps more closely associated with Teutonic rather than Anglo-Saxon design of the nineteenth century. In keeping with this character was the work of George W. & William D. Hewitt, the former having been an early partner of Furness's, and the latter a draftsman in the firm.

Willis Hale was one of the least disciplined architects of this era. Perhaps his most significant contribution was the design of hundreds of speculative row houses in North, South, and West Philadelphia (see NP I 29 and WP I 33), which seem to have become models for the character of the other work in these areas. Indeed, the extent of the popularity (and the commercialization) of this generally vulgar eclecticism in the newly developed portions of both the city and its suburbs is astounding.

Theophilus Chandler, who ultimately had a strong influence as an architectural teacher, scorned Furness's inventiveness. But while his own work was the product of a distinctly different approach to design, parallels of distortion and tension now appear evident. Chandler considered himself an academician, but his designs ultimately bear little similarity to High Victorian work elsewhere in the country.

Frequently openly parallel to Furness in design, the work of the architecture-engineering firm of The Wilson Brothers was often less bold and/or more refined. A chief competitor with Furness for the railroads' business, they should be particularly noted for their commercial and industrial designs. James Windrim, later joined by son John, was also a prosperous commercial architect, designing a number of handsome if not entirely original buildings.

Coming from Canada about 1860, Henry Sims was active in Philadelphia until his death in 1875. Henry was later associated with his younger brother James, who succeeded him. They both seemed somewhat independent of regional impressions in their approach and worked with competence and originality in new and fashionable modes from the Stick Style to the emerging Queen Anne Revival as well as the High Victorian Gothic. The bulk of their active practice, although limited to about a decade and a half, was extremely influential in introducing the quieter and more sensitive approach that was to become dominant by the late 1890s. Collaborating with them on occasion was T. Roney Williamson, who, while working with similar inclinations, fused them with the studied complexities Furness enjoyed. After a brief practice in the city, he moved to West Chester, where he practiced for a number of years, designing some of the most delightfully original work of the period in the region, much of which remains intact.

A Tasteful Creative Eclecticism

Wilson Eyre, Jr., chief draftsman for James Sims, inherited the firm upon the latter's untimely death in 1882. Soon emerging as one of the leading practitioners of the Queen Anne Revival in the country, he gave it a seldom known cohesiveness while relating it to the Philadelphia tradition of strong, simple masonry construction. Integrating the small-scale, eclectic detail and stress upon the picturesque in both plan and elevation, which were the most significant elements of the style, he added to them a unique sensibility and feeling for asymmetrical balance. Also present was a new concern for the work of the traditional artisan, not unrelated to the concurrent Arts and Crafts Movement in England. While he was the most talented, Eyre was only one of a group of young men whose work appeared in the 1880s and 90s as an exciting and more "tasteful" reaction to prevailing architectural inclinations.

Still, his earliest designs embody the overt awkwardness of Furness. If the means were different, the spirit was much the same, expressing an inherent delight in the unexpected through the intricate modeling of unlike elements. In his urban structures, like Furness and his generation, Eyre attempted consciously to break the "monotony" of the conservative neighbors, interrupting peacefully established patterns of the block. This was achieved, however, with a facade finely studied in terms of tradition and carefully related in its individuality to the buildings around it.

With his maturation, Eyre's designs became increasingly evocative of the simple and comfortable unpretentiousness of Pennsylvania rural models of the eighteenth and nineteenth centuries as well as related English prototypes. Even in the largest houses a quiet unity between building and the environment prevailed over any interest in architectural lavishness. Superb detail and balanced but not static composition of mass and interior space remained, but increasing stress was placed on the inherent qualities of materials and setting to evolve an architecture that ultimately seemed to transcend style. Such structures as the Turner House (1907) (see GM I 30) and the Townsend House in Radnor (1914) reveal this evolution of a unique design approach from a regional base that parallels the important work of Eyre's contemporary, Irving Gill, in southern California.

Eyre's principal colleagues, Frank Miles Day and partners Walter Cope and John Stewardson, although of considerable talent, never developed an equal power or personal style. More academically inclined and almost never concerned with expression of either awkwardness or complexity, they did produce a number of excellent designs in the last decades of the nineteenth century. With Eyre, they were responsible for the great monument of Philadelphia Romantic Eclecticism, the Museum of the University of Pennsylvania (begun 1893) (see WP I 10). An interesting portion of their early work, while in part derived from the Renaissance, also in some respects anticipated the spirit of the somewhat later Prairie School. Cope & Stewardson's recently demolished Harrison Laboratories at the University of Pennsylvania (1893) afforded a prime example, but by the turn of the century both firms had become well entrenched in the Beaux Arts orientation, which never really seemed to interest Eyre. However, country houses and their collegiate work, for which they were especially noted, were frequently Tudor or Jacobean in derivation, incorporating those elements that stressed the styles' informal, asymmetrical qualities. Urban designs, if more classical in origin, nonetheless retained a certain freedom and informality typical of the city, which was quite unlike the "fashionable" work in New York, Boston, or Chicago.

Horace Trumbauer's work was wholly
in the spirit of those other cities. While
the earliest buildings were executed in a
weak and reasonably standard version
of regional eclecticism, his first significant commission, an enormous "castle"
for William Harrison in Glenside (1892),
was of a scale and stylistic pretentious-
ness competitive with the contemporary
country houses of Richard Morris
Hunt. For the next thirty-five-odd
years the majority of Trumbauer's
work was to continue in this vein,
borrowing principally from English
and French Renaissance examples. The
huge palaces he erected along the Eastern Seaboard had a display of formality
and lavishness which was unusual for
the city and frequently brought scorn
from old Philadelphians. Nevertheless,
in an age of fast fortunes, he was never
without clients. In recent reevaluations
of the Beaux Arts design, Trumbauer's
significance on a national level has often
been overlooked, possibly because he
tended to keep his work within safe for-
mulas somewhat at the expense of
originality. Yet his finesse of detail and
ability to manipulate masses in proportion should place him on a par with the
best architects of the school in this
country.

The Beaux Arts and the Pastoral

In recognition of the growing national dominance of the Ecole des Beaux Arts, Philadelphia in 1903 imported one of its most promising young graduates, Paul Cret, to instruct at the University of Pennsylvania. He fit well with Philadelphia and became a leading force in planning and architecture for several decades. The Pan American Building in Washington, D.C. (1910, with Albert Kelsey) is perhaps the most noteworthy early example of his work.

But it was in the late 1920s and early 1930s that Cret was the most successful in expressing the formal statement. Through a sensitivity in the handling of mass and detail, a prevailing sense of form in the abstract transcends the materials and a certain period bias; Cret's best work has much the same quiet monumentality Strickland had achieved one hundred years before. His buildings are superbly sited, achieving a serenity that, while formal, renders building and grounds a natural whole. Beyond this, Cret devoted much effort to effecting a Beaux Arts integration of architecture and engineering. His broad scope of design included numerous bridges, dams, and even superstreamlined trains.

Other than Cret there were not many architects in the area who designed competently in the moderne. A notable exception was Ralph Bencker, who continued the work of William Price's firm of Price & McLanahan. That office had developed a strikingly original style marking a fusion of English and Sezessionist sources, which Bencker developed more fully in his commercial projects for the ubiquitous chain of Horn & Hardart restaurants and the enormous (now demolished) State Theatre (1930).

As imposing as were the Beaux Arts works in the city, they remained isolated monuments, and in an era of rapid physical expansion for Philadelphia materialized principally as conspicuous buildings in commercial centers rather than having any primary effect on the city's growth patterns. The two major products of the City Beautiful movement, the Benjamin Franklin Parkway (see CC VII 6) and the Roosevelt Boulevard, were exceptions to the body of urban development.

Concurrently, however, the influence of Wilson Eyre and several of his contemporaries began to coalesce in the work of a younger generation of architects who, like him, concerned themselves primarily with suburban domestic design and who had an enormous influence in directing the nature of the growth in these areas. While reflecting certain aspects of the shift in taste toward the academic for its own sake, they rested only on the fringe of the American Beaux Arts movement. These Pastoral architects were interested in creating an atmosphere that ultimately involved an idealization of rural life, whether that of Pennsylvania, England, or Normandy, using prototypes freely in creative and often sophisticated academic exercise. The group included Edmund Gilchrist (who had trained with Eyre but did not really carry on his primary concern for practicality before precedent), Robert McGoodwin, Mellor & Meigs, and Duhring, Okie, & Ziegler. Especially notable as an early example of their creative suburban work were the extensive speculative developments for Dr. George Woodward on his properties in Chestnut Hill (see GM II 12).

Completely unobtrusive, their buildings were nonetheless a product of an intensely creative search for natural anonymity; the extent of their ingenuity within a traditional orientation can be matched only by the best work of the Spanish Colonial Revival in southern California during the 1920s.

Ultimately the most significant member of the group was George Howe who, after working in the Furness office at a time when its meaningful existence had long passed, joined Mellor & Meigs in 1917 as a design partner. His own house in Chestnut Hill (see GM II 22), executed two years before, had already established him as a leading practitioner of the Pastoral, and with the new firm his work rapidly matured. Throughout the 1920s buildings were simplified with an increased concentration on form and its relation to the site. Yet especially in the exterior expression, the general attitude had strong similarities to that of the Shingle Style of some forty years previous. Natural materials—brick, stone, wood, and iron—were astutely contrasted in the same direct manner. Towers and complex roof patterns became as much abstract elements used to formulate a balanced but varied composition as they were picturesque attractions to charm their clients, and they also assumed a certain Mannerist distortion. Perhaps the finest of these houses was erected at Laverock for Arthur Newbold (1919-1924). The dwelling itself became only a component of a large, picturesque compound that emphasized the elements of a working farm, and although it was enormous it was completely informal.

It was during these decades of the Pastoral that literally hundreds of old farmhouses were restored and added to, and even with some of the most extensive places the simplicity of the old buildings was carefully maintained throughout. The counties surrounding Philadelphia underwent a degree of natural cultivation (in many ways similar to that of the eighteenth-century English garden) that few other rural areas in the country have chanced to experience. R. Brognard Okie was one of the first to make a scholarly study of the rural vernacular and, especially later in his career (when in practice on his own), developed the capacity to manipulate its elements as though he were an eighteenth-century master builder. His originality and creativity within these very limited boundaries were quite remarkable.

Influence of the International Style

In 1928 Howe left Mellor & Meigs and, after several months of practice on his own, joined in partnership with Swiss-born William Lescaze, who had briefly and unsuccessfully practiced in New York City. The dynamics of their six-year association is somewhat obscure, but the result was a small number of International Style buildings, the most important of which was the Philadelphia Saving Fund Society Building (1930) (see CC IV 7). This structure, built by a conservative, Quaker-dominated institution at the height of the Depression, joined the seemingly incompatible backgrounds and philosophies of the partners into a beautifully integrated statement. Their smaller work is, perhaps, more indicative of the unresolved difficulties of their partnership, suggesting that they were still groping in their attempts to express the New World Architecture. Their first commission was, in fact, the first building in the International Style in the East, the now demolished Oak Lane Country Day School (1928). A certain awkwardness, and at times contradiction, here and in other (unexecuted) jobs may also have been Howe working in a spirit close to Furness's, but of more importance was his interest in relating local materials and elements of design to modernistic principals. Once the partnership of Howe & Lescaze was dissolved, this effort was partially continued, but the quality of Howe's few commissions of this period was remarkably inconsistent. Not long after designing several rather awkward moderne residences, he produced a summer house for Mrs. C. F. Thomas in Maine which is unquestionably derived from International Style theory yet employs warm materials and a pitched roof along with details that render it in conscious sympathy with its surroundings. Such interesting and early efforts in this direction can also be found in the work of Kenneth Day, who, like Howe, had formerly designed in the Pastoral (in partnership with Edmund Purves).

The other major figure at that time was Oskar Stonorov, who was one of the first men to introduce the advanced European concepts of mass housing and urban planning to this country, designing several housing projects that were to serve as models for similar work throughout the country. They remain sensitive balances between the organization which a planner must give and the individuality and intimate scale which is desired by the inhabitants. His country houses of the thirties and forties form some of his most interesting work, with a sophistication acquired from his European training coupled with a sympathy for the landscape and understanding of the local, traditional architecture. There also exists the element of complexity, partially the result of his love for the unexpected.

Through the late 1930s, despite the quality of Howe's, Day's, and Stonorov's building, the city was basically <u>retardataire</u> in its general design ideas and in the immediate postwar period responded only vaguely to the forces that contributed to architectural innovation elsewhere in the country. After the war the three maintained generally lean practices (although Stonorov's grew sizably by the 1960s). Louis Kahn, after association with Howe and Stonorov, established his own office, producing a few searching works, but was recognized more for his role in education. Other prominent designers, Robert Montgomery Brown, George Daub, and Norman Rice, had only limited commissions. The new firm built by Vincent Kling seemed to be the only group wholly committed to the modern ethic able to secure large projects, bringing to them a number of design and engineering innovations.

If the city lacked a substantial quantity of good new architecture during the 1950s, it did have one of the most dynamic and comprehensive city plans. This was principally the creation of the then director of the City Planning Commission, Edmund Bacon, who allied his efforts with many of the city's more able architects. Oskar Stonorov and Louis Kahn made important contributions sensitive to the nature of the city and its diverse elements. Likewise, Vincent Kling, with a sophisticated organization of systems and design coordination, added significantly. Stressing practicality and taste above architectural innovation, Bacon's plans have established a pattern of quality firmly cast in the character of the city which is unusual for most mid-century urban renewal. Indeed, with maturation and a surprisingly large amount of similarly pleasant speculative work, these efforts are proving to be among the most successful in the country. But aside from the compromises apparently inherent in the realization of any significant change, the many plans for quiet and sensible neighborhood revitalization which seemed so promising an element twenty years ago generally have been forgotten. With the actual destruction of much of Southwark (see SP I 1) and the moral destruction of South Street, a less sympathetic attitude toward some of the city's assets now seems evident.

Contemporary
Development

With the 1960s, Philadelphia re-emerged as a place of significant new architecture and architectural thought with the late maturation of Louis Kahn, the arrival of Romaldo Giurgola, and Robert Venturi's start of practice. Although substantially different from one another, they share an overriding and somewhat binding attitude toward building which fits them well into the continuum of Philadelphia's past. The dominating geometric order that becomes the criterion for organization in Kahn's buildings, as well as their monumental solidity, seems an aspect evolving from his training with Paul Cret. However, unlike Cret but shared with Furness is the recognition that architectural statement need not always be in either beautiful or simple terms. Not unrelated is Venturi's interest in redefining contemporary vernacular architecture without violating its frequently ugly qualities. While the unifying elements in his work are not always immediately apparent, there is a pervading simplicity of the dominant mass and individual detail which has a directness and austerity that relate to the indigenous Quaker tradition. This interest in studied complexities subordinated to a quiet, simple whole is not dissimilar in spirit to the work of Wilson Eyre and his successors in redeveloping an anonymous farm architecture in the first decades of this century. Romaldo Giurgola, while less involved with a rigidly defined philosophy, is more integrative of divergent attitudes, reflecting both his contemporaries and elements of Philadelphia tradition.

The influence of these men has been evidenced more in general stimulation of the work of others than in a significant collection of their own buildings. Kahn, though idolized by many students and critics, has scared many in the city with a reputation for gross impracticality, and amidst his honors glares the fact that he has not had a major commission built in Philadelphia for a decade. Venturi likewise has been limited to only minor work in the city, and Giurgola is only beginning to receive conspicuous commissions. But a number of other architects are now expressing a decisive interest in their work, even if in execution they often fail to capture the integrity of the ethic with which they have become allied. A considerable amount of the new construction and design of the past several years seems to reflect this new attitude. If calling this phenomenon the "Philadelphia School" is a bit overenthusiastic, there is nonetheless a suggestion of the emergence of a vital, and once again widely practiced, regionalism not dissimilar to that evident during creative periods of the past.

The scope of contemporary architecture in the city extends, of course, well beyond these limits. Both the firms of Geddes, Brecher, Qualls & Cunningham and Bower & Fradley share a certain sympathy with such work, yet their buildings usually express a more direct and essentially simple clarity. The resulting conservative dignity is even more consciously apparent in the work of Vincent Kling, whose office continues to produce many of the larger buildings in the area and has been instrumental in keeping the general level of commercial and civic development at a high standard of integrity and taste. Carroll, Grisdale & Van Alen have worked toward a more openly eccentric but not unrelated concern. While there has been no large body of significant domestic design in the Philadelphia area over the past twenty years, a number of offices have done some notable residential work. Cope & Lippincott along with Montgomery, Bishop, & Arnold have done modern work with a clear appreciation of the early local traditions. Louis Sauer displays the rare ability to give a "wide" appeal to imaginative, livable, and distinctively personal residential design, often of a multiunit type. Frank Weise has been conducting interesting architectural experiments for the past twenty years and has produced some of the more fascinating houses in the area.

Likewise, Joel Levinson, while just beginning his practice, is part of no school but a source of tasteful and inventive works.

The patterns of architectural and urban development of the city are intricate and exceedingly complex; no attempt has been made even to summarize them here. Further research, particularly in the work of the past one hundred years, is needed before an accurate depiction of such events can be attempted. Essential to such progress is a well-founded knowledge of the buildings themselves and of the environments they help to create, and it is toward this end that the following pages are devoted.

**Center
City**

The limits of Philadelphia as set down by William Penn, and existing until the consolidation of the city and county in 1854, were from above Vine Street to South Street, river to river, the area long known as Center City. It has always maintained a position of importance in the greater metropolitan area comparable with its central location, and predictably it contains the most varied, interesting, and largest concentration of buildings of architectural interest. While no small number of significant works have been demolished, even in recent years, a good representation of over two centuries of both good civic and commercial structures exists within a relatively small area. In addition, a large portion of the downtown sector has remained in low-density residential use, forming pleasing and often dramatic changes in scale as well as allowing retention of a large group of houses.

The eastern end of Center City is the oldest and has undergone the most extensive changes in recent years. These have often, for better or worse, become models for renewal in other communities nationwide. The waterfront had been used almost entirely for commercial purposes during the previous century. In the 1950s it became a focal point for the city's rejuvenation with the development of the Independence National Park and Society Hill. Pioneering in both concept and scale, they have been the new "image givers" for the city and have triggered a large amount of tasteful private rehabilitation and development.

The Independence National Park has preserved a number of historically and architecturally important buildings of the eighteenth and early nineteenth centuries. In addition to demolishing a number of equally if not more important buildings of later decades, however, the planning made the tragic mistake of assuming that good works of urban architecture should best exist in a park setting. Still the transformation was well scaled, creating a varied east-west axis from Independence Hall to the too-large-for-demolition Customs House. A few ersatz Georgian buildings have been added, and there are threats of more.

The most unfortunate addition to the area is the oversized, underscaled Independence Mall by the Commonwealth of Pennsylvania, whose dimensions and position make it difficult to ignore.

Settled under a grant to the Free Society of Traders in 1682, Society Hill incorporates an unparalleled collection of recently rehabilitated Georgian, Federal, and Greek Revival houses and has attracted pleasant and often excellent new residential development. It should be cited as the first large urban area to be renovated for low-density residential use.

The remaining portion of the downtown waterfront has been little touched in this century, and although it contains a few Georgian remnants it consists primarily of Greek Revival and early Victorian mercantile loft structures. Many of these buildings are excellent representatives of types that have become virtually extinct in most cities in the country. Regrettably there is no plan for preservation of the district, and the generally decaying state of the buildings places the future of these blocks under speculation.

Residential areas continue from Society Hill west to the Schuylkill River, between Locust and South Streets, and cover the spectrum of nineteenth-century residential development and twentieth-century redevelopment. Although over the years many of the large houses on the western blocks of Locust and Spruce Street have gone from one-family dwellings to elaborate apartments and offices, their fabric and context have been well maintained. Smaller houses on Pine and Lombard Streets and adjacent alleys have seen some years of neglect, but hundreds have undergone major rehabilitation. Restoration of old streets such as Camac was begun in the first decade of the century, and small new developments followed in the ensuing years, but the most extensive rejuvenation dates from the last decade. The back alleys are especially delightful and their extent is rather surprising. Occasional new and creative housing has added considerable visual richness.

The main thoroughfares for shopping and business are Market, Chestnut, and Walnut Streets. In the last twenty-five years many companies have moved from the east to the west side of Broad Street, leaving the blocks to the east filled with commerce of a less stylish nature. East Market Street has lost little of its life if it has lost its polish and is the projected site of a major attempt at downtown revitalization. Streets to the north host a myriad of commercial supply houses in a handsome assortment of late-nineteenth-century lofts. Among them lies one of the last burlesque houses in the country as well as a small untouristed Chinatown.

The western blocks of Market, Chestnut, and Walnut, if more fashionable, still possess a hectic juxtaposition of buildings. It is not uncommon to find properties that have been completely rebuilt several times in this century adjacent to buildings well over a hundred years old. Rittenhouse Square, in part, epitomizes this lack of regularity and demonstrates that it can be interesting as well as a source of visual confusion.

An impressive unification does occur around City Hall Square and south on Broad Street, where for several blocks large skyscrapers relate formally to the flamboyant Public Buildings. Penn Center to the west extends this homogeneity at the expense of vitality. In concept it dates to the 1920s, when several schemes were proposed for the Pennsylvania Railroad by Graham, Anderson, Probst & White, Daniel Burnham's successors. With the exception of the Suburban Station, buildings were not erected before the mid-1950s, and then from an entirely different plan. While certainly not the modernists' answer to Rockefeller Center as it was heralded as being, work has mostly been inoffensive and civic in scale. A more stimulating civic effort was the Benjamin Franklin Parkway of half a century before. A great diagonal opening into the city's gridiron pattern from City Hall to Fairmount Park, its total execution brought the Beaux Arts tendency toward broad scale and somewhat academic formality into a delicate balance with the character of the rest of the city, creating a most pleasant, humane, and adaptable sector.

**Center
City I**

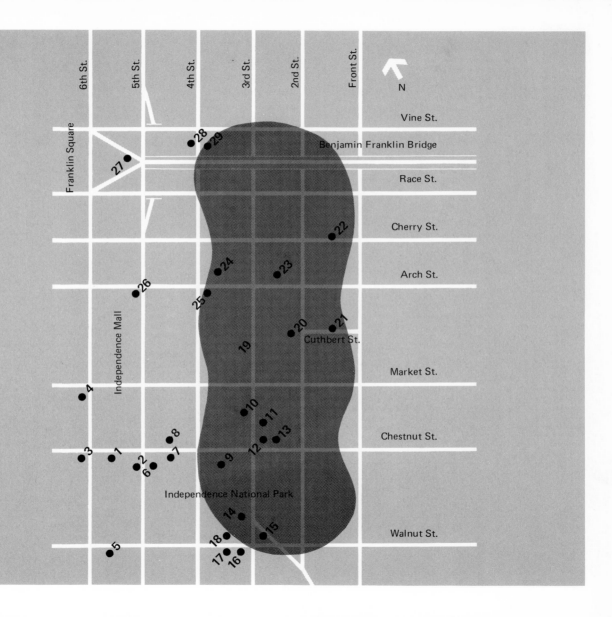

CC I

1
Old Governmental Group

Chestnut Street, between 5th and 6th Streets
Open to the public

1 A
The State House of the Province of Pennsylvania (Independence Hall)

Ca. 1730-1748, Edmund Woolley and Andrew Hamilton. Tower 1753; frame portion of tower removed 1781; tower rebuilt along slightly different lines 1828, William Strickland. Wings rebuilt 1811, Robert Mills; demolished in restoration 1895. Assembly Chamber "restored" 1831, John Haviland; "restoration" for the Centennial Celebration 1872; further restorations 1897, T. Mellon Rogers, and 1920s, Horace Sellars; archeological restoration 1956 to date, National Park Service

1 B
County Courthouse (Congress Hall)

1787; 1793

1 C
Old City Hall (Supreme Court Building)

1790, David Evans, Jr.

What is probably the earliest planned group of civic buildings in the country has endured a century and a half of "preservation," forming a fascinating history of the evolution of interest in Colonial architecture. The National Park Service has spent one-tenth of that time trying to undo what previous generations did.

2
American Philosophical Society Building (Philosophical Hall)

1785-1791; third floor added 1890, removed 1950
104 South 5th Street, Independence Square

The gaunt Federal wrapping is an unassuming cover for one of the nation's foremost and oldest cultural institutions.

3
Public Ledger Building

1924, Horace Trumbauer
6th and Chestnut Streets

Georgian detail is carefully restrained in a dignified and well-proportioned mass that, together with the less cohesive Curtis Publishing Company Building (Edgar Seeler, 1910), forms a compatibly urbane border to the west side of Independence Square.

4
Rohm and Haas Building

1964, Pietro Belluschi (Cambridge) and George Ewing & Company (Alexander Ewing, designer)
6th and Market Streets, SW corner

5
Penn Mutual Life Insurance Company Building Additions

1970-1974, Mitchell/Giurgola Associates
Incorporating the facade of the Pennsylvania Fire Insurance Company Building 1838, John Haviland; east portion and cornice 1901, Theophilus Chandler
6th and Walnut Streets, SE corner

The massive addition to the company's headquarters (Edgar Seeler, 1913; Ernest Matthewson, 1931) reflects Guirgola's current interest in the interaction of glass curtain wall and concrete surface. The facade of the Egyptian Revival landmark, reconstructed following careful dismantlement, is handled as a thin planar object.

6
American
Philosophical
Society
Library
(Library Hall)

1954, Martin, Stewart & Noble
127 South 5th Street

A reproduction of the facade of Dr.
William Thornton's 1789 Library
Company of Philadelphia

7
Second Bank
of the
United States

1818-1824, William Strickland; mid-
nineteenth-century alterations, John
McArthur, Jr.; restored to 1818
condition
420 Chestnut Street
Open to the public

In the early nineteenth century the
numerous Greek Revival structures of
this neighborhood provided a monumentality and order, serving as visual
focuses for the generally unpatterned
cityscape much as ecclesiastical and
civic buildings had done earlier.

8
Bank Row

8 A
Lafayette
Building

1907, James H. Windrim; altered
5th and Chestnut Streets

8 B
The Pennsylvania
Company
for Insurance
on Lives
and Granting
Annuities

1873, 1880, Addison Hutton
431 Chestnut Street

8 C
Farmers and
Mechanics Bank

1855, John Gries
427 Chestnut Street

8 D
Bank of
Pennsylvania

1857, John Gries; alterations 1900,
Theophilus Chandler
421 Chestnut Street
Now Philadelphia National Bank

8 E
Philadelphia
National Bank

1898, Theophilus Chandler
323 Chestnut Street

8 F
First
National Bank

1865, John McArthur, Jr.
315 Chestnut Street

Part of the old financial center, these
structures formed one of the more
notable groupings of Mid- and High-
Victorian buildings in the city. Many of
the finest have become only history,
including Frank Furness's Provident
Life and Trust Company (1876-1879).

CC I

9
Carpenters'
Hall

1770-1775, Benjamin Loxley and
Robert Smith
Chestnut Street, above 3rd
Open to the public

The Carpenters' Company remained
the dominant influence in building design through the eighteenth and well
into the nineteenth centuries. Even so,
its headquarters was modestly set in a
small court at the end of an alley rather
than on a main street. The siting is
vaguely reflected in the new landscaping
by the two reproductions built in front
of it.

10
Mechanics
National Bank

1837, William Strickland; additions
1874, James H. Windrim
22 South 3rd Street
Now Norwegian Seamens' Church

11
Leland
Building

1855, Stephen Button
37-39 South 3rd Street

The industrial frankness of the contemporary loft building was skillfully related to more formal architectonics in
one of the finest works of this commercial architect.

12
C. L. Borie
Counting House

1896, Wilson Eyre, Jr.
3rd and Chestnut Streets, NE corner

13
Group
of Lofts

13 A   Ca. 1854, Joseph Hoxie
Leland Building   235 Chestnut Street

13 B   1854, Joseph Hoxie
Elliott Building   237 Chestnut Street

13 C   Ca. 1856, Stephen Button
Stores   239-241 Chestnut Street

14   1795, Samuel Blodgett, Jr.; banking
First Bank   room 1901, James H. Windrim
of the   120 South 3rd Street
United
States

An early American attempt to exploit
what was considered to be full "classical" regalia, it met with impressive results and created a formal terminus to
Dock Street, once a busy commercial
center. As with the Second Bank, it is
barely complimented by its new surroundings.

CC I

15
Philadelphia Exchange

1832, William Strickland; altered 1900, Louis Hickman; exterior restored and interior altered
3rd and Walnut Streets, NE corner
Now National Park Service offices

The free arrangement of Greek elements responding to the irregular site reveals a flexibility not generally associated with the Classical Revival.

16
The Pennsylvania Company for Insurance on Lives and Granting Annuities

1859
304 Walnut Street

17
Philadelphia Saving Fund Society

1839, Thomas U. Walter; pediment added 1881, James Sims; altered
306 Walnut Street

18
Houses
300 Block of
Walnut Street

18 A
Bishop White
House

Ca. 1780
309 Walnut Street
Open to the public

18 B
William
McIlvaine
House

Ca. 1793
315 Walnut Street
Now National Park Service offices

18 C
Charles Hare
House

1809
321 Walnut Street
Now National Park Service offices

18 D
Twin
Houses

Ca. 1812
323-325 Walnut Street
Now Pennsylvania Horticultural Society

18 E
Dilworth-Todd-
Moylan
House

Ca. 1775
343 Walnut Street

339-341 are total reconstructions of
houses of the same date.

Admirably restored houses have been
joined by new construction to form the
only segment of the National Park that
relates to the former urban landscape.

Between Walnut Street and Vine, from Front Street to 4th, lies one of the city's most important and most neglected architectural areas. Only New Orleans and New York still contain mid-nineteenth-century commercial districts of comparable size and interest. That which was built here is considered to be of key significance in the evolution of a commercial "style" that later culminated in the work in Chicago of the 1880s and 1890s. Virtually all the most important single examples of these buildings were demolished over ten years ago by the National Park Service. What remains, however, is important as an area.

The number of Greek Revival lofts that survive is remarkable. Front Street, from Walnut to the Benjamin Franklin Bridge consists almost entirely of these pre-Civil War structures. 30, 32, 111 to 123 North 3rd Street are also good examples. Romantic variations on these, many with an abstracted Gothic second story, are prevalent; 138-140 Front Street is perhaps the best example, with rusticated stone and simple, beautifully cut cornices. 10, 12, 36, 38, 51, 54, 56, 58, 120-126 North 3rd Street are simpler versions. There are many good Italianate fronts both in cast iron and stone. The 200 block of Chestnut Street is one of the finest groups. 28 North 3rd Street is an elaborate variation once common to the district.

Little is known about the designers of these buildings. Hoxie and Button, who were considered to be important commercial architects, inevitably were responsible for a number. 242-244 Delaware Avenue is known to have been designed by them, and their influence, along with that of Samuel Sloan and other contemporary architects, can be seen throughout the area, 233 North 2nd and 225 Race being good examples. 135-137 North 3rd Street, while full of architectural flourish, shows little of the usual structural frankness. 60-66 North 3rd is similar but of such a size that it appears more as a hotel than a commercial loft. 61-63 North 3rd and 101-111 Arch Street have very elaborate cast-iron facades. In sharp contrast 113-115 Market Street is composed merely of the simplest structural articulation between large areas of glass.

The number of lofts dating from the High-Victorian era is not as extensive. 56-60 North 2nd Street has interesting Queen Anne detailing. 121-123 Market (The Wilson Brothers, ca. 1883) is a simple brick loft quite similar to many found in comparable districts of New York. 309-313 Arch is of a much larger scale than most in this section, and is of a type still readily found to the west of Independence Mall.

CC I

20
Christ Church

1727-1744, probably by John Harrison and John Kearsley; tower and steeple, between 1751 and 1754; rebuilt 1771, Robert Smith; interior alterations 1833, Thomas U. Walter
North 2nd Street, above Market

A remarkable ecclesiastical structure for its time, Christ Church remains one of the most significant Georgian churches in the country. The lavish use of Palladian forms found here was not uncommon in pre-Revolutionary Philadelphia for important civic structures, churches, and large country houses.

21
Coomb's Alley

After 1759, Jacob Cooper and Henry Harrison, carpenters
112-118, 124 Cuthbert Street

While this sector of the city has long served a commercial function, several groups of eighteenth-century houses have managed to survive.

23
Houses
200 Block of
Arch Street

23 A House	Before 1753 219 Arch Street
23 B House	Before 1754 221 Arch Street
23 C Betsy Ross House	Before 1765; additions 239 Arch Street Open to the public

24
Loxley Court

1741, Benjamin Loxley, carpenter
On north side Arch Street above 3rd

22
Elfreth's Alley

Various dates between 1724 and 1836
100 Block Cherry Street

Elfreth's Alley remains one of the few
blocks in the city reflective of the early
eighteenth-century townscape and retains many of the oldest extant houses
in the city. Number 126 is open as a
museum.

25
Arch Street
Friends
Meetinghouse

1803-1811, Owen Biddle; additions
1968, Cope & Lippincott
4th and Arch Streets, SE corner

The Quakers' architecture forms a significant aspect of the characteristics of regional design. As with many of the early meetinghouses that remain in the city and surrounding areas, this is a superb study in simple, direct expression of form and material.

26
Free Quaker
Meetinghouse

1783
5th and Arch Streets, SW corner

27
Delaware River
(Benjamin
Franklin)
Bridge

1919-1926, Paul Cret; Ralph Modjeski, chief engineer, George Webster and Lawrence Ball, associate engineers Approach at North 5th Street between Race and Vine

No small portion of Cret's eminence came from his ability to integrate the Beaux Arts ethic with works of engineering. What was, at its time of construction, the longest suspension bridge in the world remains a singularly impressive entrance to the city.

28
**Saint
Augustine's
Church**

1848, Napoleon LeBrun
North 4th Street, below Vine

Built following anti-Catholic riots that
destroyed its predecessor, Saint Augustine's is an interesting Victorian adaptation of elements of Georgian design and
helps illustrate LeBrun's originality.
Much of the detailing has been removed
from the tower.

29
**Saint George's
Methodist
Church**

1763-ca. 1770
235 North 4th Street

**Center
City II**

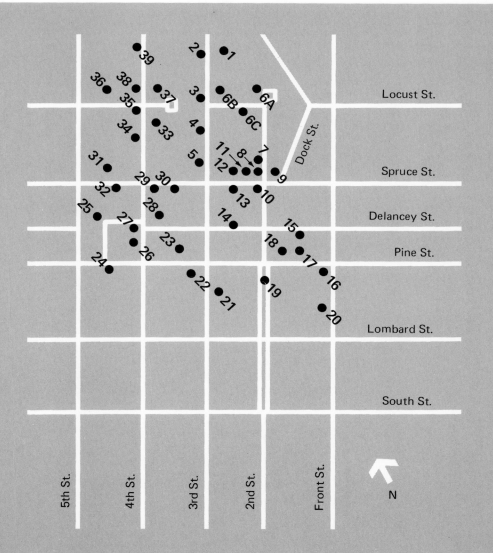

CC II

1
Saint Paul's
Church

1761, William Dilworth, carpenter;
alterations 1830, William Strickland
225 South 3rd Street
Now Children and Family Service

Contrasted with the simplicity of the
Quaker meetinghouses, Saint Paul's
seems more to "lack ornament."
Strickland's large doorway may have
been intended to give the facade focus.

2
Winder Houses

1843-1846
232-234 South 3rd Street

3
Samuel Powel
House

1765, for Charles Stedman
244 South 3rd Street
Open to the public

Restored before the Second World
War, the Powel House was the first
dwelling in the area to receive such attention and provides an excellent illustration of large Georgian city houses
in Philadelphia. As was generally the
case, the interiors were as elaborate as
the street facade was simple.

4
Michael Bouvier
Houses

1849
258-262 South 3rd Street

5
Houses

Ca. 1814, James Lyndall and Joseph
Antrim, builders
268-274 South 3rd Street

6
Dock Street
Superblock

6 A
Society Hill
Towers

1964, I. M. Pei & Associates (New York)
Locust and 2nd Streets

6 B
Society Hill
Town Houses

1962, I. M. Pei & Associates
Locust and 3rd Streets, NE corner

6 C
Town Houses

1969, Louis Sauer Associates
Locust Walk, between 3rd and 2nd
Streets

The initial group of apartments served
as a well-publicized impetus to attract
many who had deserted the city. Such a
conspicuous focus was, indeed, probably essential in selling the idea of urban
rehabilitation to a skeptical public.

CC II

7
Captain James Abercrombie House

After 1758
268-270 South 2nd Street
Now Perelman Antique Toy Museum

A dwelling of dimensions that were still considered to be quite large for city houses of one hundred years later, it further illustrates the magnificence attained in the city at an early date.

8
Samuel Neave House

Between 1758 and 1765
272-274 South 2nd Street

9
Man Full of Trouble Inn, 1759
Benjamin Paschall House, 1760

2nd and Spruce Streets, SE corner
A museum open to the public

The city's oldest surviving tavern has been left uncomfortably alone by redevelopment. It was just off Dock Creek, originally conceived of as the center of town.

10
Southern Loan Society/ John Sailor House

After 1837; ground floor redesigned with restoration 1968, Magaziner & DiGiorgio
300 South 2nd Street

One of the better remaining Greek Revival town houses in the city, its recent alterations are well in keeping with the character of the original.

11
James Davis
House

ca. 1760, James Davis, carpenter; additions 1780s for David Lenox
217 Spruce Street

12
Henry Watts
House

1961, George B. Roberts
219 Spruce Street

Few of the Neo-Georgian attempts in the last decades have been especially successful. This house, whose apparent size is deceptive, stands as an interesting exception, incorporating inventive elements yet not deviating from the character of design of the late-eighteenth century.

13
Philip Winemore
and
William Arbow
Houses

Ca. 1743-1746; remodeled into one house 1958
220-222 Spruce Street

CC II

14
200 Block
Delancey Street

14 A Alexander Barclay House	1758 217 Delancey Street
14 B Houses	1756, John Goodwin, builder 214-216 Delancey Street
14 C Franklin Roberts House	1969, Mitchell/Giurgola Associates with Roy Vollmer 230 Delancey Street
14 D Drinker House and Court	Ca. 1766 241 Pine Street and behind to Delancey Street

14 E West-Grandon Houses	Ca. 1794 242-244 Delancey Street
14 F Houses	Ca. 1768 246-248 Delancey Street

An unusually fine block of houses that contains many examples of the best surviving simpler Georgian city architecture.

15
Eli Zebooker
House and
Office

1968, Mitchell/Giurgola Associates
110-112 Delancey Street

Here the prevailing Georgian scale and proportion of the street is defied with much the same enthusiasm the High-Victorian architects enjoyed.

16
Group of Houses

1970, Louis Sauer Associates
Pine and Front Streets, SW corner

17
Alan Halpern
House

1965, Wallace, McHarg, Roberts & Todd
113 Pine Street

Recent work by some of the city's most interesting architects has rendered Society Hill a far more stimulating neighborhood than would have been the colonial confection desired by some.

18
James
McClennen
House

1967, Louis Sauer Associates
127 Pine Street

[51]

CC II

19
Head House
Square
Area

19 A
Head House
and Market

1804, market 1745
2nd Street, from Pine to Lombard

19 B
Head House
Square
Development

1966, Frank Weiss
West side 2nd Street
1973, Louis Sauer Associates
East side 2nd Street

19 C
Central Penn
National Bank

Late-nineteenth century; reconstruction
1967 George B. Roberts
2nd and Pine Streets, NW corner

The commercial focus of Society Hill
incorporates primarily older structures
skillfully adapted for a variety of contemporary uses. The market originally
extended to South Street with a like
firehouse at this other "head."

20
Reed Houses

Ca. 1812
518-520 South Front Street

Well evident here is the strength of the
Georgian design that persisted long after
the Revolution.

21
Kellogg House

1968, Hans Egli
415 South 3rd Street

22
Saint Peter's
Church

1758-1761, Robert Smith and John Kearsley; steeple 1842, William Strickland
South 3rd and Pine Streets, SW corner

Built at a time when travel for more than a few blocks in the city posed a considerable problem, Saint Peter's was designed for parishioners of Christ Church who lived in the immediate area. Fortunately the interior has never experienced an extensive remodeling and still contains many of its Georgian furnishings.

23
Robert
Blackwell
House

Between 1805-1816
313 Pine Street
Now Saint Peter's Church Rectory

24
Third
Presbyterian
Church

1767, Robert Smith; extensive alterations 1837; remodeled 1857, John Fraser; remodeled 1867; restored to 1857 design 1955
Pine Street, between 4th and 5th

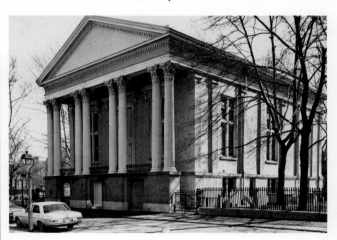

CC II

25
Lawrence Court

1968, Bower & Fradley
Cypress Street, above 4th

26
Thomas Neval House

1771, Thomas Neval, carpenter
338 South 4th Street

A small house built by a well-known carpenter for himself enjoys decorative devices of an elaboration generally found on larger dwellings.

27
Nancy Grace House

Restorations and additions to the 1782 Moses Bussey House 1968, Stonorov & Haws
320 South 4th Street

A crystalline pavilion in a walled garden was added to the restored house in a manner reminiscent of Stonorov's earlier work bridging the eighteenth and twentieth centuries in Chester County.

28
Hill-Physick-Keith House

1786; alterations 1815
321 South 4th Street
Open to the public

The sole survivor of numerous free-standing Federal and Greek Revival town houses that once graced the city, the Physick House has been restored as a museum with its garden replanted in the spirit of the early nineteenth century.

29
Wharton House

Before 1796
336 Spruce Street

30
Houses
for the
Stephen Girard
Estate

Probably 1832
326-334 Spruce Street

One of many speculative rows for the
estate throughout the older sections of
the city. Essentially Federal houses,
these were classicized in keeping with
the fashion by surfacing the ground-
floor fronts with marble.

31
400 Block
Spruce Street

31 A
House

1792, William Williams, carpenter
425 Spruce Street

31 B
House

Ca. 1790, William Williams, carpenter
427 Spruce Street

31 C
House

Between 1791-1795
429 Spruce Street

31 D
House

1803
431 Spruce Street

32
First
Spruce Street
Baptist Church

1830; facade 1851, Thomas U. Walter
418 Spruce Street
Now Society Hill Free Synagogue

While detailing is Romantic in origin,
the eclectic mixing of styles and of large
scale is entirely Mid-Victorian pretension. The design called for two large
towers that would measurably have
aided the effect.

33
Houses

Ca. 1812, Jacob Vodges, carpenter
253-257 South 4th Street

34
Saint Mary's
Church

1763; additions 1811, Charles Johnson;
alterations 1886
252 South 4th Street

Perhaps inspired by Latrobe's Philadelphia Bank (1807, demolished 1836), the master carpenter Johnson gave Saint Mary's a Gothick facade that was inevitably imposing for its day. It has long been the earliest work in the style remaining in the city. Among later interior alterations was an organ by T. U. Walter (1839).

35
Alterations
for the
Mutual Assurance
Company

1913, Stewardson & Page; altered.
Combining the Joseph Norris (Cadwalader) House 1828 and the Casper Wistar House 1798.
4th and Locust Streets, SW corner

An agreeable conversion of two houses into offices for one of the country's oldest insurance companies helps illustrate that sensitivity to the city's eighteenth-century elements is hardly a recent interest.

36
Houses

1802-1807, Peter Berry, carpenter
413-415 Locust Street

37
Bingham Court

1967, I. M. Pei & Associates
4th Street at Locust Street

An elegant grouping of houses that, like
a number of other recent developments,
takes full advantage of the Philadelphia
tradition of alleyways and courtyards.
This even incorporates an earlier prototype, Bell's Court (ca. 1814).

38
Houses

1801-1804
226-232 South 4th Street

These four dwellings provide an interesting contrast of stylistic approaches current in the early 1800s.

39
**The Philadelphia
Contributionship
for the
Insurance of
Houses from
Loss by Fire**

1835, Thomas U. Walter; fourth floor
added 1886, Collins & Autenreith
212 South 4th Street

Although built for the Contributionship,
this early office building followed closely on the pattern of free-standing city
houses of the era.

**Center
City III**

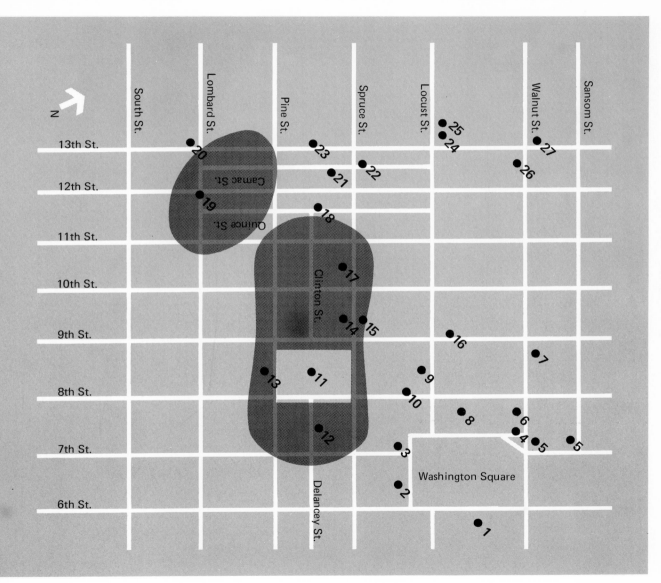

CC III

2
Hopkinson
House

1962, Stonorov & Haws
Washington Square South

Long interested in perfecting the design of high-rise apartment houses, Stonorov was able to produce a handsome, efficient, yet unostentatious focus for the rehabilitation efforts commencing concurrently to the south of the Square.

3
Washington
Square
Houses

3 A
Asaph Stone
House

1818
700 Washington Square South

3 B
Houses

1818
702-708 Washington Square South

The remnants of Federal Philadelphia that are scattered throughout this area have often been regarded with somewhat less admiration than they deserve. If not as spectacular as comparable dwellings in Boston and New York, they were by no means undistinguished. Many have been admirably restored.

1
The Athenaeum
of Philadelphia

1845, John Notman
219 South 6th Street

Notman's English training enabled him to introduce a number of stylistic "advances" to this country. Somewhat patterned after Sir Charles Barry's Travellers' Club in London, the Athenaeum was a key building in the formulation of an urban Italianate mode for eastern cities.

4
Philadelphia
Saving Fund
Society

1868, half of center pavilion 1883, Addison Hutton; half of center pavilion and west pavilion 1897, Furness, Evans & Company; alterations and vault rooms 1930, Howe & Lescaze
7th and Walnut Streets

Furness's contribution lies mainly inside with the creation of a huge banking hall supported by appropriately proportioned arches. It was the company's main offices until its building at 12th and Market Streets proved to be worthy of the move.

5
Speculative
Houses for
William Sansom

1799, 700 block Walnut Street (north side), Benjamin Latrobe; 700 block Sansom Street (south side), Thomas Carstairs

While not the first row in the city, this was one of the largest for its time and apparently quite influential on ensuing work. 701 Walnut was rebuilt as a handsome brownstone loft (1855). 724 Sansom is also of a later period and sometimes attributed to Frank Furness.

6
York Row

1807, Joseph Randall, carpenter
712-716 Walnut Street

More in keeping with the stylistic norms of the Federal period, what remains of the row reveals that it was one of the city's more elegant. Most of the later development that was not derived from Sansom Row seems to have been inspired by it.

7
Walnut Street
Theatre

1809, enlarged 1811; remodeled 1828, John Haviland; altered ca. 1850, Joseph Hoxie and Stephen Button; interior remodeling 1903, Willis Hale; interior remodeling 1920, William H. Lee; facade restored to 1828 appearance, interior remodeled and enlarged, 1970 John Dickey and Bryan Loving

Thought to be the oldest theater in continuous operation in the English-speaking world, it is the last of a number of legitimate houses that flourished in the early decades of the previous century when Philadelphia was a theater center. Adapted once again to contemporary needs, its future seems secure.

8
Luke Wistar
Morris
House

1787, built by William and John Reynolds; rear additions, late nineteenth century
225 South 8th Street

The double-lot house was unusual in the city prior to the nineteenth century. The street front here has never seen alteration, and, as with the Mutual Assurance Company, the additions to the rear were respectful of the original.

9
Musical Fund Society Hall

1824, William Strickland; enlarged 1847, Napoleon LeBrun; rebuilt with new facade 1893, Addison Hutton; altered 806 Locust Street

10
Saint Andrew's Church

1822, John Haviland
256 South 8th Street
Now Greek Orthodox Cathedral of Saint George

If perhaps the most nearly correct classical paradigm erected in the city, the church possesses little of the monumentality of more interpretive works like the Second Bank.

11
Pennsylvania Hospital

East Wing, ca. 1755; West Wing, ca. 1796, both from a 1751 design by Samuel Rhoads; Central Pavilion 1794-1805, David Evans, Jr.; numerous later additions
Pine Street, between 8th and 9th

The oldest hospital in the country, its siting results in a pleasing, unexpected break in the city's narrow street patterns. The Center Pavilion has long been regarded as one of the finest Federal structures in the country. The pedestal for the cast-iron statue of William Penn in the front yard was designed in 1804 by Benjamin Latrobe, who also may have done the handsome brick walls on Pine Street.

12
Spruce and Pine Streets

The blocks of Spruce and Pine Streets west of Society Hill contain a large number of fine Federal and Greek Revival town houses that, if not primary examples, are handsome remnants of the period and vital contributors to the character of Center City. Most are of considerable size and pose no small problem for rehabilitation. Some have been taken over for institutional use, but many remain in a bad state of repair. The 900 and 1000 blocks of Clinton Street are some of the handsomest in this area and have also managed to remain some of the best maintained.

13
John Eisenbrey, Jr., House

1850, Hoxie & Button
814 Pine Street

Notman was clearly not the only Philadelphian working early and significantly in Brownstone. The tasteful Greek exterior elements are complemented by an interior rich with the exotic imported woods of the client's business.

14
Portico Row

1831, Thomas U. Walter
South side of Spruce Street, from 9th
to 10th

15
Carolina Row

Between 1812 and 1815, attributed to
Robert Mills; altered
925, 929-933 Spruce Street

16
Franklin Row

1809, Robert Mills; later alterations
228 South 9th Street

Using the simple, monumental forms
common to the grand English rows of
the period, Franklin Row was probably
the first group in Philadelphia to be
handled as a cohesive architectural entity rather than a compilation of individual units. Only one of the eleven houses
now stands, and it too is threatened
with demolition.

The preceding generation's desire to break up the seemingly monotonous Federal rows was shared by Eyre and his contemporaries, as shown here. The row at 1101-1115 Spruce Street (Brown & Day, 1889) is another agreeable example.

18
Mask and Wig
Clubhouse

Remodeled as club 1894, 1901, Wilson Eyre, Jr.
310 South Quince Street

Altered from an 1834 church turned stable, the building has an outstanding Craftsman interior, graced with Maxfield Parrish murals.

17
Rodman Wistar
House

1887, Wilson Eyre, Jr.; all but upper facade removed 1965
1014 Spruce Street

One of Eyre's early experiments in reducing a building's composition to a very limited number of essential components arranged in an unorthodox yet sensible manner. Clearly inspired by late medieval urban dwellings in northern Europe, it is reflective of the growing interest in anonymous architecture as precedent.

19
Twelfth and
Lombard Streets
Area

19 A   1965, Frank Weise
Washington Mews 11th Street and adjoining parts of
Lombard and Rodman Streets

19 B   1968-1971, Alan Klein (New York)
Macedonia Place 1124-1134 Lombard Street

19 C   1968, Francis, Cauffman, Wilkinson &
Horizon House   Pepper
501 South 12th Street

19 D   1963, Frank Weise
Camac Village   1201-1217 Lombard Street, 423-429
Camac Street

19 E   1966, Geddes, Brecher, Qualls &
Houses   Cunningham
1107-1113 Pine Street and rear on
Panama Street

Private interests have brought about extensive rehabilitation of the residential areas west of Washington Square between Locust and South Streets in the past ten years. Much of the work has encompassed construction of new row houses and apartments as well as conversion of existing structures. While some of the designs are compromises, and execution at times displays cheapness, many of the projects have been positive additions to their neighborhoods. The preceding are perhaps the more interesting results of this development.

20
Casa Fermi Apartments

1962, Stonorov & Haws
13th and Lombard Streets

21
Camac Street

The blocks of this alley between Walnut and Pine Streets contain some of the earliest in-town rehabilitation. Beginning shortly after the turn of the century a number of the buildings on the 200 block were converted into clubs; those on the 300 block were retained as houses. In addition to being one of the more charming of Center City's back streets, it set an important precedent that has continued on a large number of similar secondary streets and alleys.

22
Theodore Etting House

1892, Frank Miles Day
1219 Spruce Street

Day's academic inclinations are momentarily subdued in a simple design that bears some kinship with the free Romanesque of John Wellborn Root and others in the Midwest as well as Hartwell & Richardson in Boston.

23
Saint Luke and Epiphany Church

1839, Thomas Stewart; interior alterations, 1898, Charles M. Burns, Jr.; interior alterations 1906, Wilson Eyre, Jr.; parish house ca. 1873, Furness & Hewitt
330 South 13th Street

24
Joseph Leidy House and Office

1894, 1896, 1897, Wilson Eyre, Jr.; altered
1319 Locust Street
Now Poor Richard Club

26
St. James
Apartment House

Ca. 1900, ca. 1904, Horace Trumbauer
13th and Walnut Streets, SE corner

Trumbauer's pretentious eclecticism,
then fashionable in New York, made
his work fairly distinguishable in Philadelphia and popular with those eager
to display their wealth. For this conspicuous building in a once very fashionable neighborhood, he exercised little
restraint in exhibiting his architectural
convictions.

27
Philadelphia
Club

1838; addition 1888, Furness, Evans &
Company
13th and Walnut Streets, NW corner

Thought to have been built as a house
for Thomas Butler, it must have been
one of the most splendid of the period,
although the style is somewhat retar-
dataire.

25
Clarence Moore
House

1890, Wilson Eyre, Jr.
1321 Locust Street

The variety of materials and detail, beautifully expressed and well integrated in
a delicately balanced asymmetrical
composition, were more typical of the
architect's work at this date than the
approach used in the Wistar House (CC
III 8). The restraint employed when
working with this complexity was perhaps Eyre's greatest ability.

**Center
City IV**

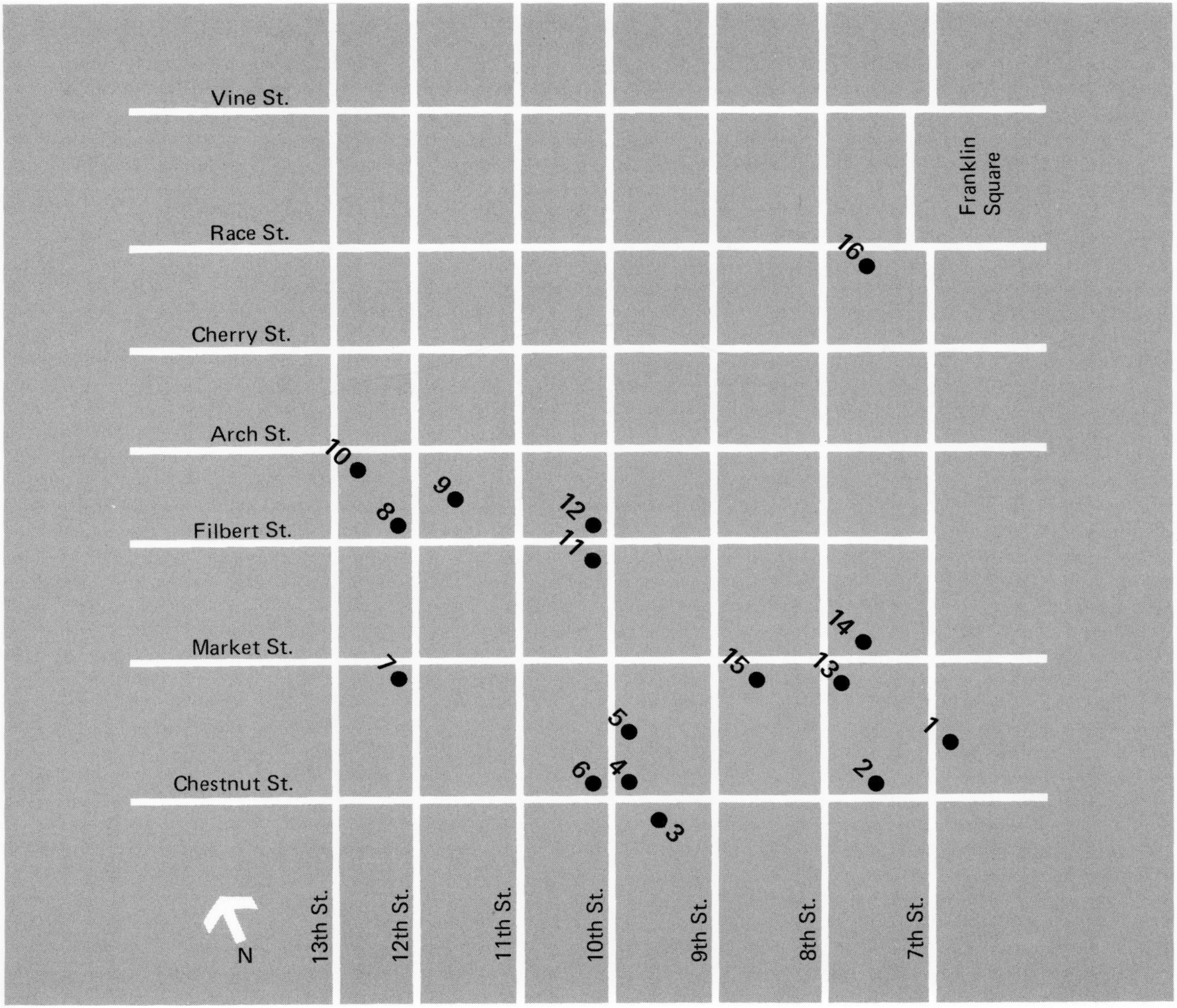
Vine St.
Race St.
Cherry St.
Arch St.
Filbert St.
Market St.
Chestnut St.
Franklin Square
13th St.
12th St.
11th St.
10th St.
9th St.
8th St.
7th St.
N
1
2
3
4
5
6
7
8
9
10
11
12
13
14
15
16

2
**Union Trust
Company**

1888, Willis Hale
713 Chestnut Street

Less than a third of the original pile
(later renamed the Quaker City Bank)
remains. The juggling of forms and tex-
tures, if undisciplined, is perhaps Hale
at his best.

3
Dunbar Block

1853, Stephen Button
920-922 Chestnut Street

1
**Franklin
Institute**

1825, John Haviland
15 South 7th Street
Now Atwater Kent Museum

Haviland's interest and ability in working with abstracted classical elements is
well exemplified in this remarkably austere and effective little building.

4
Federal Reserve Bank

1931-1935, east wing and garden 1940, Paul Cret; later additions
10th and Chestnut Streets, NE corner

Cret's superior understanding of proportion in both basic form and detail was matched by the restraint he exercised in applying Beaux Arts principles, giving his works a vitality closely related to classic origins. His contemporaries, although aiming for a modern classicism, often produced such bulky works as the adjoining Federal Building (1937).

5
Saint Stephen's Church

1822, William Strickland; decorations 1851, Richard Upjohn (New York); interior alterations and transept 1878, Frank Furness; Parish House 1888, George Mason, Jr.
19 South 10th Street

Although Strickland designed a number of nonclassical buildings, he never appeared to be comfortable in these more divergent modes.

CC IV

6
Mutual
Insurance
Company
Building

1873, Henry Fernbach (New York);
altered and three floors added 1890,
Phillip Roos (New York); addition 1902
10th and Chestnut Streets, NW corner
Now Victory Building

The last survivor of a formidable group
of bombastic financial structures that
once lined these blocks of Chestnut
Street.

7
Philadelphia
Saving Fund
Society
Building

1930, Howe & Lescaze; television tower
1948, Louis E. McAllister and Douglas
Braik
12th and Market Streets

A principal landmark in the evolution
of the skyscraper, it was the first devoid
of popular fashion or connotations of
the past. In a rare moment, Lescaze's
charming but period-oriented moderne
is transcended by a timeless quality that
retains today its stature as a great work
of art and an extremely well working
office building. The organization of
space, dictated in part by economics,
was a radical departure from the image

of the banking house but bears comparison to Ritter & Shay's contemporary Market Street National Bank (1929, altered) nearby at Market Street and Penn Square. PSFS's huge escalator and banking rooms rank among two of the city's finest spaces. A serious visit should not exclude the office entrance on 12th Street and some typical office floors.

8
PSFS Garage

1931, Howe & Lescaze; altered
12th and Filbert Streets

An early instance of a large parking facility built in conjunction with a single office building, it has suffered considerable defacement.

9
Philadelphia and Reading Terminal Shed

1891, The Wilson Brothers
12th Street, Cherry to Filbert Streets

Lying to the rear of an undistinguished station building whose facade by Francis Kimball (New York) is besieged with seedy twentieth-century "improvements," this magnificent and now rare piece of nineteenth-century engineering will sadly be razed if the Market Street East project sees realization. The Terminal Market on the street level is a survival of earlier train-oriented commerce and remains a food center of some repute. A fine Horn and Hardart automat by Ralph Bencker is located on Market Street.

CC IV

10

A. J. Holman
Stores and
Factory

1881, The Wilson Brothers
1222-1226 Arch Street

As yet unaltered, this provides a fine example of increasingly scarce High Victorian commercial structures throughout the immediate area.

11
Firehouse

1850s; altered
10th and Filbert Streets, SW corner

Interesting in its use of Egyptian Revival detailing on an otherwise unremarkable structure.

12
Loft Building
for
C. C. Harrison

Ca. 1890, Cope & Stewardson
10th and Filbert Streets, NW corner

The sensitivity of the firm's work is well displayed in a fusion of free academic eclecticism with the commercial frankness common to contemporary work in Chicago. The adjoining store building at Northwest 10th and Market Streets was also by the firm (1893).

13
8th Street
Subway Entrance

1970, Mitchell/Giurgola Associates
8th and Market Streets

14
Lit Brothers
Store

One section ca. 1850; Baily Store 1873; 8th Street end for Lit Brothers 1893, Collins & Autenreith; alterations to 715-721 Market Street and 7th Street end 1898, Collins & Autenreith; alterations and additions
North side of Market Street, 7th to 8th Streets

One of the finest and last remaining blocks of nineteenth-century mercantile facades, many in cast iron, the complex grew through a series of adaptations and construction that still resists precise documentation.
  Incorporated at the rear is another loft, at 714-718 Arch Street (James Windrim, 1881).

15
Gimbel Brothers
Store

(East to west) Gimbel Building 1900, Francis Kimball; Sharpless Building; Weightman Building 1888, Willis Hale; Haines Building 1893, Addison Hutton; rear sections added; alterations
South side of Market Street, 8th to 9th Streets

A somewhat heavier and later commercial aggregation than Lit Brothers. The fine addition to the Strawbridge and Clothier Store at 8th and Market Streets, NW corner, by Simon & Simon (1928) also bears note.

16
Police
Administration
Building

1963, Geddes, Brecher, Qualls & Cunningham
Race Street, between 7th and 8th Streets

Little that is commonly associated with the police station can be found in this ingenious prestressed concrete building.

**Center
City V**

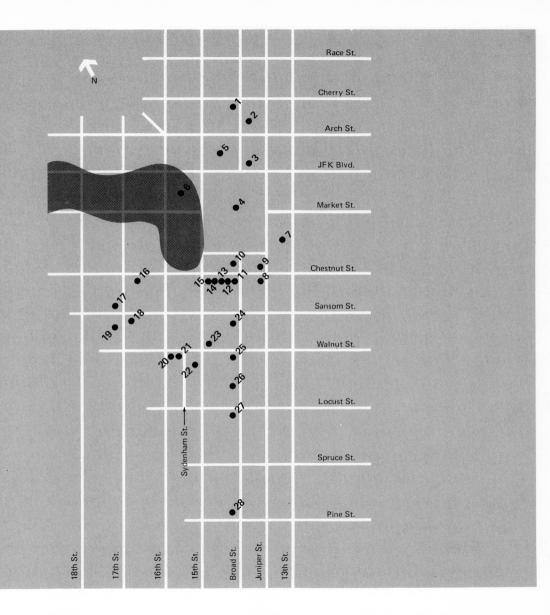

1
Pennsylvania Academy of the Fine Arts

1871-1876, Furness & Hewitt
Broad and Cherry Streets

A combination academy and museum, it is probably Furness's best-known work and was doubtlessly instrumental in firmly establishing his reputation. The building's dual role is bluntly expressed with a huge, highly ornate stair and exhibition hall leading logically into a series of unadorned galleries; the teaching studios are tucked beneath these on the first floor.

2
Philadelphia Life Insurance Company Annex

1963, Mitchell/Giurgola Associates
125 North Broad Street

3
Masonic Temple

1868-1873, James H. Windrim
Broad and Filbert Streets
Public tours

What is essentially a Romantic style is appliqued on too large a building, with surprisingly successful results. The interior by George Herzog is rendered with even more vigor, each lodge room in a different "exotic" style.

**4
The Public
Buildings
(City Hall)**

1871-1901, John McArthur, Jr.
(Thomas U. Walter, consulting),
Alexander Milne Calder, sculptor
Penn Square
Public tours

One of the most extraordinary products of an era that was known for temerity in design, City Hall deserves study in proportion to its size. Although stylistically well within the realm of Second Empire work by A. B. Mullet and other contemporary architects, there is none of the usually sought-after delicacy that was at once Mullet's strength and weakness, nor is any pretension achieved through the traditional great flight of stairs leading to the main entrance. Indeed, there is no main entrance, rather four large arches opening a simple courtyard to the city. While the interior boasts of a number of enormous and dutifully elaborate chambers, there is no great entrance hall or gallery as was usually the standard for the era. City Hall's overpowering monumentality is the result of its strong form and carefully proportioned scale, which remain the omnipresent elements in the design despite the phenomenal accumulation of decoration. The tower, too, is scaled to maintain its stature as a dominant feature in the skyline at some distance. It is one of the very few civic structures in the country to attain symbolic monumentality corresponding to its purpose.

John Ord became supervising architect on McArthur's death and is thought to have designed much interior detailing.

CC V

5
Municipal
Services
Building

1964, Vincent Kling & Associates
Broad Street and John F. Kennedy
Boulevard

What was one of the most difficult sites
in the city has been skillfully developed
so that it possesses civic dignity, yet
does not vie with the eclectic profusion
of buildings that surround it.

6
Penn Center

1956-
Market Street to John F. Kennedy
Boulevard, west of 15th Street

One of the first-planned, multiblock,
high-rise office building complexes in
the country, in concept Penn Center
dates back to the 1920s. The existing
plan, however, did not begin to take
form until after the Second World War.
While much of this planning was mud-
dled with revisions and compromises,
at times the work of the Pennsylvania
Railroad (the actual developer), it was
pioneering in its scope and amenities.
  The initial stages of building by Emery
Roth & Sons (New York) and Vincent
Kling succeeded in providing neither a
sense of urbane dignity commonly associated with such a center nor an informal series of humane open spaces coor-
dinated with the buildings. Later work
such as Kling's IBM Building (1963) has
been generally more responsive. Kling
has been responsible for a large share of
the building in the Center in addition to

the overall planning and open space, and
he has begun to attain the sophisticated
formality that would have been a dominant element in a large business center
built before the Second World War. In de-
liberate contrast is MurphyLevyWurman's
Banking Hall for the Industrial Valley
Bank (1968) and to some extent Kling's
own recent Centre Square (1973), an

excellent two-building development set
asymmetrically about a diagonal axis,
framing a complex enclosed space suggestive of a shopping mall.

   Although the total complex can still be
criticized for its core of blandness and
"dead" space, with the exception of
the structures fronting John F. Kennedy Boulevard, it has achieved a tasteful
cohesiveness rare in most downtown
urban renewal schemes.

7
John Wanamaker
Store

1902-1911, D. H. Burnham & Company
(Chicago) with John T. Windrim
Market to Chestnut Streets, 13th to
Juniper Streets

Burnham's grandly scaled but essentially
simple functional plan has made this
one of the most enjoyable department
stores in the country. The great central
court (complete with organ) has few
peers.

8
Keystone
National Bank
Building

1887, 1890, Willis Hale
Juniper and Chestnut Streets, SW corner
Now Hale Building

9
Widener
Building

1914, Horace Trumbauer; alterations
1963
South Penn Square and Juniper Street
to Chestnut Street

Stormy protests spared the north facade
from the same tasteless remodeling given
the Chestnut Street front. Subsequent
renovations in Center City have generally been more sympathetic.

**10
Girard Square**

Girard Trust Company Building, 1905, McKim, Mead & White (New York) and Allen Evans of Furness, Evans & Company; north wing 1923, 1931, McKim, Mead & White; Morris Building, 1910, Furness, Evans & Company; Fidelity Mutual Life Insurance Company Building, 1969, Vincent Kling & Associates
Broad to 15th Streets, Chestnut Street to South Penn Square

**11
Land Title
Building**

1897, 1902, D. H. Burnham & Company; ground floor alterations 1964, Vincent Kling & Associates
Broad and Chestnut Streets, SW corner

The older section is a good representative of the firm's noted early work, especially interesting when contrasted with the more academic addition done five years later. Kling's renovation was reflective of a growing appreciation for the integrity of past design.

12
Cooper
Jewelry Store

1959, Geddes, Brecher & Qualls
1416 Chestnut Street

A sophisticated "gem" whose interior is understated elegance.

13
Crozer Building—
American
Baptist
Publication
Society

1899, Frank Miles Day & Brother; altered
1420-1422 Chestnut Street

Despite the negative comparison with the Land Title Building (see CC V 11), Day's free eclectic design of 1896, with its pleasant arcade, displayed a gentle sensibility that marked the better local work of the era.

14
Jacob Reed's
Sons
Store

1903, Price & McLanahan
1424 Chestnut Street

One of the earliest reinforced concrete buildings not used for a simple industrial purpose, its vaguely Byzantine facade relates to the University Museum (see WP I 10).

CC V

15
**Packard
Building—
Pennsylvania
Company
for Insurance
on Lives
and Granting
Annuities**

1924, Ritter & Shay
15th and Chestnut Streets, SE corner
Now First Pennsylvania Bank

Part of a conservative league that formed
much of the core of what most remem-
ber as "downtown," its effectiveness
cannot be dismissed as anything less
than successful in generating the concept of the city as a place of importance.

16
WCAU Building

1935, Gabriel Roth (Harry Sternfeld,
design consultant); altered
1620 Chestnut Street

Originally painted blue and silver, this
was Philadelphia's prime piece of
"radioland" moderne.

17
**Stock Exchange
Building**

1965, Vincent Kling & Associates
17th and Sansom Streets, NW corner

18
**First Baptist
Church**

1898, Edgar Seeler
17th and Sansom Streets

Romanesque Revival found little popularity in Philadelphia, and this somewhat
indecisive structure was, perhaps, its
best representative here.

19
Houses

Ca. 1885, Furness & Evans
130-132 South 17th Street

Oversized elements are tamed and played against an otherwise simple mass in what was originally a group of five houses. The ability to employ this type of restraint was vouchsafed to few of Furness's contemporaries.

20
Integrity
Trust Company
Building

1928, Paul Cret; altered
1528 Walnut Street
Now Fidelity Bond & Mortgage Company

21
John Anglee
House

Before 1858, style of John Notman; altered
Sydenham and Walnut Streets, SE corner
Now Sydenham Building

If not designed by Notman, this sophisticated brownstone house was doubtlessly influenced by his work including the Tait House, which formerly stood across Sydenham Street.

22
1500 Walnut Street Building Additions

1963, Bower & Fradley
15th Street below Walnut

A richly detailed sympathetic addition to Ritter & Shay's former First National Bank Building (1928)

23
Drexel and Company Building

1927, Charles Z. Klauder
15th and Walnut Streets, NE corner

Florence, almost—and really an anachronism for its time; perhaps it will not prove too difficult an assertion for contemporary use.

24
The Union League of Philadelphia

1864, John Fraser; interior alterations 1889, Charles M. Burns, Jr., Theophilus Chandler, George Herzog, and James H. Windrim; annex 1911, Horace Trumbauer
Broad and Sansom Streets to 15th Street

25
Bellevue-Stratford Hotel

1902, 1909, G. W. & W. D. Hewitt; 1913, Hewitt & Paist
Broad and Walnut Streets, SW corner

The largest and most splendid hotel in the city when completed, it was representative of the increasing lust for uninhibited opulence which marked virtually all of the great hostelries of the period.

26
Art Club

1893, Frank Miles Day & Brother; additions ca. 1909, Newman & Harris
220 South Broad Street

Together with the Union League and the Academy, this delicately rendered building gives an essential human scale to the tall office blocks of South Broad Street.

27
American Academy of Music

1855, Napoleon LeBrun and Gustave Runge
Broad and Locust Streets·

LeBrun's proposed Victorian Baroque design for the exterior was never realized, and the simple but dignified "temporary" front has remained. The main effort went into creating the rich and acoustically superb auditorium that surpassed most expectations.

28
Deaf and Dumb Asylum

1824, John Haviland; wings 1838, William Strickland; additions 1854; rear additions 1874, Furness & Hewitt
Broad and Pine Streets
Now Philadelphia College of Art

An unusual assemblage of work by nineteenth-century brutalists, it was to have been extensively added to by one of the twentieth, Louis Kahn.

**Center
City VI**

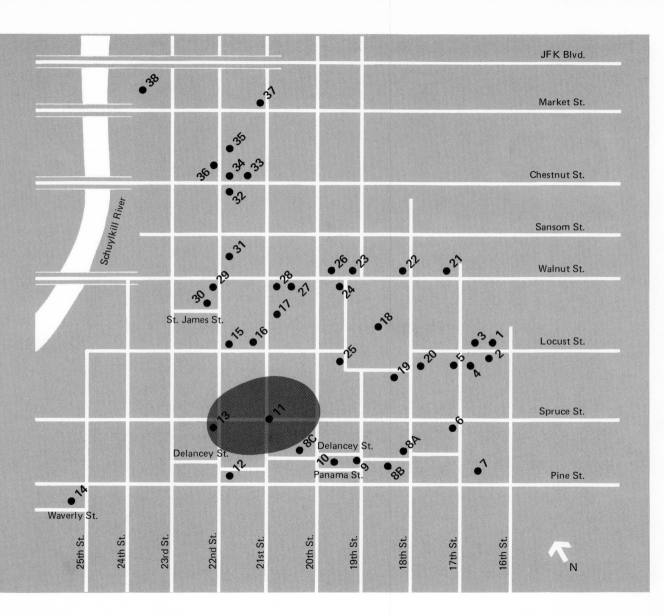

2
Early Houses
1600 Block
Locust Street

2 A
John Converse
House

Alterations to an earlier house 1897,
The Wilson Brothers; interior, George
Herzog; alterations 1900, Baily &
Truscott
1610 Locust Street

2 B
Henry Dallett
House

Ca. 1850, John Notman; alterations for
C. C. Harrison 1888, Wilson Eyre, Jr.
1618 Locust Street

1
Saint Mark's
Church

1847-1851, John Notman; Clergy House
1893, Hazelhurst & Huckel; Lady Chapel
1899, Cope & Stewardson; embellished
1625 Locust Street

One of the earliest "correct" and mature
Gothic ecclesiastical works in the country. Notman seems to have been responsible for the present design although
plans were originally submitted by the
English architect R. C. Carpenter.

2 C
House

Ca. 1850, John Notman; altered
1620 Locust Street

2 D
House

Ca. 1860
1622 Locust Street

The simplicity and finesse of Notman's pioneering brownstone work can still be discerned. 1622 Locust Street is typical of the elaboration that ensued in later developments of the style. At 1618 the delicate ability to respect the essence of the original while still injecting a new and lyric statement marks Eyre's alteration for Harrison.

3
Later Houses
1600 Block
Locust Street

3 A
Edward Knight
House

1902, Horace Trumbauer
1629 Locust Street

3 B
Double House
for
A. C. Harrison

1895, Cope & Stewardson
1631-1633 Locust Street

3 C
Carlton Yarnall
House

1908, Frank Miles Day & Brother
17th and Locust Streets, NE corner

3 D
John Markoe
House

1901, Cope & Stewardson
1630 Locust Street

Trumbauer's infatuation with showy Parisian eclecticism is in marked contrast with the others' quiet but concerted effort to blend the academic with design traditions more consistent with the city.

4
Double House
for
Edward Wood

Ca. 1890, Frank Miles Day; altered
245-247 South 17th Street

5
Harry Lewis
House

1894, W. Whitney Lewis (Boston);
recent alterations
242 South 17th Street

Designed by one of the Back Bay's most
prominent architects, its similarity of
approach to contemporary Philadelphia
work rather than to that of the Boston
area is deserving of note.

6
West Spruce
Street
Presbyterian
Church

1854, John McArthur, Jr.; spire
removed
17th and Spruce Streets
Now Tenth Presbyterian Church

Orange brick and iron ornament are
combined in a handsome and vigorous
Lombard pastiche.

7
Frank Weise
House

1955- , Frank Weise
307 South Chadwick Street

Situated on one of the many rejuve-
nated back streets, the building's dramatic spaces contain both home and
office.

8
Delancey Place

8 A
Joshua Husband
House

1857
1801 Delancey Place

8 B
H. Labarre Jayne
House

1895, Wilson Eyre, Jr.
1824 Delancey Place

8 C
Maurice Speiser
House

Remodeled 1933, George Howe
2005 Delancey Place

From 17th Street west, this forms one
of the city's most attractive streets. The
1800 block is, perhaps, the most impressive, lined with tall Federal town
houses, built mostly in the 1850s, which
provide interesting evidence of how long
Georgian design survived in the city.
The various blocks were staggered pur-
posefully to discourage through traffic.

The change in scale between them is
also worth noting. The 1700 and 1900
blocks principally contain carriage
houses, and the 2100 block has residences of a similar size. The grander
scale of the 1800 block is resumed west
from 20th and 22nd Streets.

9
Horace Jayne
House

1895, 1899, Furness, Evans & Company
320 South 19th Street

Seemingly unusual as a product of the
Furness office, this and the Harrison Day
Nursery at 19th and Ellsworth Streets
(1899) suggest some of the more restrained variations of its work.

10
Panama Street
Development

Ca. 1922, George W. Pepper, Jr., Charles
Borie, and William Koelle
1900 block of Panama Street

An early rehabilitation effort making
use of a former alley, it is lined with
picturesque post-Arts and Crafts houses.

CC VI

**2000-2100 Blocks
Spruce Street**

Many of the most interesting houses in this area are located along Spruce Street and in particular in these two blocks. The entire district has suffered little change in this century and forms an extremely attractive residential enclave that should be the recipient of positive steps to ensure that its integrity is not marred. The parallel blocks of Locust Street are of interest as well, although the general effect is less unified. There are numerous alleys such as Van Pelt Street, where small houses and stables have been skillfully adapted for present-day use.

2002-2012 and 2009-2021 Spruce Street are austere brownstone Italianate rows representative of numerous houses still extant in center city. 2016 is similar stylistically but is a double house. 2023-2045 are of slightly later date, using Eastlake ornament. 2036-2038 are sparingly detailed for the period, attaining their effectiveness through form. 2040 is a late Second Empire house with High Victorian ornament. 2047 and 2100 (by G. W. Hewitt) are extremely simple, following the example of some of Furness's better work. 2101 is a very elaborate, rectilinear Italianate villa of a ponderousness similar to the William Vanderbilt houses in New York designed by Charles Atwood. 2113 is the Rudolph Ellis House by Furness & Hewitt (ca. 1874), later altered in 1889 by Furness, Evans & Company for R. Winder Johnson. 2123 was remodeled in 1900 for D. Webster Dougherty by Wilson Eyre, Jr., in a very discreet Georgian. 2132-2134 reduces many typical Philadelphia High Victorian idioms almost to caricature. 2137 is a handsome essay in rectilinearity and of a restraint unusual for the period.

12
Neil and Mauran Houses

1891, Wilson Eyre, Jr.
315-317 South 22nd Street

13
Holy Trinity Memorial Chapel and School

1874, James Sims
22nd and Spruce Streets

Iron flying buttresses and glass curtain wall mark an unusual variation on the Gothic.

14
Anne Tyng House

Remodeled 1967, Anne Tyng
2511 Waverly Street

An interesting addition to an anonymous back-street house that reflects Kahn's influence and Tyng's spatial talent. This area has been the object of no small rehabilitation effort executed along pleasingly modest lines.

16
Mrs. John Neill House

1889, Wilson Eyre, Jr.
2103 Locust Street

17
Thomas Hockley House

1875, 1894, Furness & Hewitt
235 South 21st Street

Probably Furness's most interesting extant urban dwelling, it also deserves comparison with the adjacent four houses at 21st and Locust Streets which are probably a later (ca. 1888) Furness product.

15
John Bell House

1906, Horace Trumbauer
22nd and Locust Streets, NE corner

Trumbauer's Neo-Georgian designs usually avoid the ostentatiousness so common in much of his work. Even with an increase in scale, he seems to have been careful to preserve the proportions that were so important to the essence of the original.

18
Rittenhouse
Square

Remodeling 1913, et seq., Paul Cret
Walnut to Locust, 18th to 19th Streets

One of the most pleasant open spaces
in the city, Cret's improvements attain
a subtle balance of urbane enhancement
without violation of the park's natural
character.

19
House

1891, George Casey (of Furness, Evans
& Company)
1804 Rittenhouse Square

The textural possibilities of cut stone
are fully exploited in a fashion not unusual for the period in Philadelphia.

20
Samuel
Wetherill, Jr.,
House

1909, Frank Miles Day & Brother
251 South 18th Street
Now Philadelphia Art Alliance

CC VI

21
House

1890, Frank Miles Day; later alterations
1707 Walnut Street

22
Alexander
Van Rensselaer
House

1899, Peabody & Stearns (Boston)
1801 Walnut Street

23
Rittenhouse
Plaza
Apartments

1924, McLanahan & Bencker
1901 Walnut Street

One of the most effective of the early skyscraper apartments on the square which combine to form a background architecture that is especially important in establishing an identifiable urban atmosphere.

24
Church
of the
Holy Trinity

1856-1859, John Notman; tower 1868, additions and parish building 1890, W. D. Hewitt; alterations 1898, Cope & Stewardson; altered
Walnut Street and Rittenhouse Square West

For so prominent a site and congregation, Notman executed a church of appropriate monumentality, quite distinct in approach from the more intimate character of Saint Mark's (see CC VI 1). As with his contemporary, Richard Upjohn, he proved to be accomplished not only in various ecclesiastical modes but in relating them to existing surroundings.

25
Rittenhouse
Dorchester
Apartments

1964, Milton Schwartz & Associates
226 West Rittenhouse Square

26
Thomas McKean
Houses

1897, Cope & Stewardson
1921-1923 Walnut Street

27
James Scott
(John Wanamaker)
House

1882, Theophilus Chandler
2032 Walnut Street

While Chandler considered himself an academic, his buildings were seldom without a flagrance distinctly High Victorian in character. Walnut Street was once lined with a number of grand houses, another of which, by the same architect, is at 2006 Walnut Street (1888).

28
Second
Presbyterian
Church

1869, Henry Sims; chapel 1884, style of Theophilus Chandler; one-story addition to chapel and tower 1900, Furness, Evans & Company
21st and Walnut Streets
Now First Presbyterian Church

The tower forms a fitting terminus to a High Victorian Gothic work that stays just on the tasteful side of inventive excess.

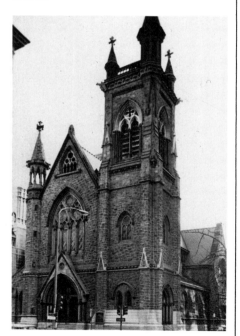

29
House

1877, Addison Hutton and John Ord; interior alterations 1899, Horace Trumbauer
22nd and Walnut Streets, SW corner

30
Houses

Ca. 1880, attributed to Frank Furness
2203-2203½ St. James Street

Both sides of this block of St. James Street contain a notable assemblage of little altered High Victorian houses.

31
**100 Block
South 22nd
Street**

**31 A
Hutchinson
House**

1882, Theophilus Chandler
133 South 22nd Street

**31 B
Thomas
Cochrane
House**

1882, G. W. & W. D. Hewitt
125 South 22nd Street

**31 C
Robert Lewis
House**

Ca. 1886, attributed to Frank Furness
123 South 22nd Street

The Brown Decades at one of their least restrained moments, these houses suggest the degree to which architects in Philadelphia were revolting from the tradition of harmonious, indeed often identical, adjoining buildings. Much of the immediate neighborhood once consisted of similar endeavors.

**32
Bradsbury
Bedell
House**

1889, Wilson Eyre, Jr.; altered
22nd and Chestnut Streets

The facade at once awkward and extremely refined, seemingly random and yet finely balanced, was wholly beyond precedent and represents one high point in the urban work of Eyre's early years.

**33
First Unitarian
Church and
Parish House**

1884, Furness & Evans; altered
2125 Chestnut Street

Executed for the congregation of which his father was minister, it is exemplary of the individuality the preacher so vehemently proclaimed. The peculiar corner tower as well as the heavy rustication and some ornament have not survived the years.

34
Church of the
New Jerusalem

1881, 1902, 1907, Theophilus Chandler
22nd and Chestnut Streets

Chandler's notion of a peaceful sanctuary was felt to be "ruined" with the erection of the Furness church next door. The use of open space and subsidiary buildings is quite accomplished.

35
College of
Physicians

1908, Cope & Stewardson
19 South 22nd Street

36
Saint Anthony
Club House

1888, Wilson Eyre, Jr.
32 South 22nd Street

37
Erlanger
Theatre

1928, Hoffman-Henon Associates
21st and Market Streets, NW corner
Now Café Erlanger

A rare survivor of the theater's golden age. The firm was a leading designer of motion picture houses in the city; its tour de force was the Mastbaum, which once stood a block to the east.

38
Philadelphia
Electric
Company
Building

1970, Harbeson, Hough, Livingston & Larson
23rd and Market Streets, NW corner

**Center
City VII**

Pennsylvania Ave.

Benjamin Franklin Pkwy.

Calowhill St.

Wood St.

Vine St.

Winter St.

Race St.

Cherry St.

Arch St.

Schuylkill River

N

23rd St.

22nd St.

21st St.

20th St.

19th St.

18th St.

17th St.

16th St.

CC VII

1
Saint Clement's Church

1855-1859, Parish School 1864, John Notman; decorations 1864, Richard Upjohn (New York); alterations and additions 1901, Horace Sellars; steeple removed
20th and Cherry Streets, NW corner

2
Gulf Oil Station

Ca. 1925
20th, and Arch Streets, SW corner

A proportionately small number of these neighborhood filling stations remain serving their original function. Their designs were generally pleasant, appropriately unobtrusive, and were of a scale that was agreeable to most communities.

3
Prentiss Building

1970, Carroll, Grisdale & Van Alen
19th and Arch Streets

Color has been astutely employed to relate this building to the unfortunate but too-large-to-hide neighbors that front John F. Kennedy Boulevard.

4
YWCA Building

1891, Benjamin D. Price
1800 Arch Street
Now Philadelphia College of Bible

Designed by a noted Philadelphia delineator, this is an unusual instance of the direct influence of the Chicago School in the city.

5
West Arch Street Presbyterian Church

1850-1855, Joseph Hoxie; towers removed
18th and Arch Streets, SE corner

With a vigorous free mixing of styles, the church remains a powerful eclectic statement, a success Hoxie seldom enjoyed in his noncommercial work.

6
Benjamin Franklin Parkway

The result of efforts starting as early as 1884 to reconstruct a gridiron city pattern into something of the image of the City of Light, the great axial avenue, stretching from City Hall to Fairmount Park, placed on the city maps in 1903, was studied by such men as Cret, Eyre, Kelsey, Medary, Trumbauer, and Frenchman Jacques Gréber, who prepared the final designs in 1917. This final solution bears a surprising resemblance to Lutyen's plan for New Delhi, begun a few years previous. Construction of the project started in 1917 and took only two years to complete.

The great street was to be lined with a collection of imposing public edifices. Most never materialized, but the Art Museum and the buildings around Logan Square suggest something of the architectural expectations.

Rather than planning on strictly uniform cornice lines, unity was achieved through strong axiality enhanced by rows of trees resulting in a strong cohesion even today with the variety of structures that now front it. The street furniture and lampposts (most now replaced) done by Paul Cret in 1925 additionally helped to enrich the character of the boulevard.

Fitting Logan Square into the scheme was a major problem solved by cutting a circle in it. This is judiciously treated as a low, landscaped park focused upon the tasteful Swann Memorial Fountain

(1924) by Wilson Eyre & McIlvaine and Alexander S. Calder. The view is thus not entirely obstructed, only interrupted, giving depth to the vista.

Graced by two strong focuses and good topography with sufficient space, the Parkway must be considered one of the country's finest urban spaces, even though recent years have seen incompatible alterations to enhance traffic flow adjacent to the museum.

7
United Fund
Building

1969, Mitchell/Guirgola Associates
Race Street and Benjamin Franklin Parkway

The building's scale and articulation reflect a sensitive understanding of the Parkway. What at a distance appears as a dignified if modest office building is revealed, on close inspection, to be a highly inventive mannerist study in the formal concept of the curtain wall.

8
Cathedral of Saints Peter and Paul

1846-1851, Napoleon LeBrun; facade and supervision 1851-1857, John Notman; completed 1857-1864, Napoleon LeBrun, with Fathers Maller and Tornatore; additions and alterations 18th and Race Streets

LeBrun's attempt at academic grandeur has been somewhat eclipsed by later Parkway buildings. While the exterior was never completed to his plan, the interior (with works by the painter Brumidi) is doubtless a manifestation of his concept of the whole.

9
American Society for Testing and Materials Building

1964, Carroll, Grisdale & Van Alen 1916 Race Street (Logan Square)

The difficult problem of appropriately relating a building of so small a frontage to the square has been impressively solved, in what was then a unique solution. Rear portions of the structure are in the full spirit of Philadelphia eccentricity.

10
Free Library of Philadelphia

1917-1927, from a 1908 design by Horace Trumbauer
Vine Street, between 19th and 20th

Trumbauer's outright plagiarism is amazingly effective as integrated into the entire Parkway plan. The other structure built in conjunction with his scheme is the adjoining Family Court Building by Morton Keast, built in 1938-1941 (from 1931 plans of John T. Windrim). John T. Windrim's Franklin Institute (1934), the School District of Philadelphia Administration Building by Irwin Catherine (1930), and the Boy Scouts Building by Charles Z. Klauder (1929) carried on the development somewhat more freely.

11
Youth
Study Center

1953, Carroll, Grisdale & Van Alen
20th Street and Pennsylvania Avenue,
SW corner

The standard institutional image is abandoned with a creative use of dynamic spaces enhanced by a diversity of natural materials, for what was to be an enlightened juvenile detention facility as well as a Parkway monument.

12
Rodin Museum

1929, Paul Cret and Jacques Gréber
22nd Street and Benjamin Franklin
Parkway, NE corner

13
Fairmount Park
Guards'
Guard House

Ca. 1860; moved from East River Drive,
1972
Benjamin Franklin Parkway and The
Crescent (23rd Street)

14
**Philadelphia
Museum of Art**

1916-1928, Charles Zantzinger, Horace Trumbauer, and Charles Borie
Benjamin Franklin Parkway and Spring Garden Street

Although sited in Fairmount Park, the museum is of the Parkway. First regarded by many as a defiant intrusion to the park, its very power is what has made the building an irreplaceable fixture.

15
**Fidelity Mutual
Life Insurance
Company
Building**

1926, Zantzinger, Borie & Medary
26th Street and Fairmount Avenue (at Pennsylvania Avenue)
Now part of the Museum of Natural History

Fairmount
Park

Fairmount Park, oldest and one of the largest city parks in the nation, began with the landscaping of the grounds of the "new" waterworks at the foot of Fair Mount in 1812. The results met with sufficient favor to justify a series of substantial expansions, and through the nineteenth century some 4000 acres were acquired. Much of this land consisted of large country places fronting the Schuylkill River. Fortunately, many of the numerous Georgian and Federal houses located there were incorporated into the new park, forming what is now regarded as an incomparable collection of rural domestic architecture of the period. No other city in this country has been able to spare so large an open area of so early a date with its houses intact. The largest places are open to the public as extremely fine period museums; the numerous smaller dwellings serve a variety of uses.

While much of the park today is the product of astute Romantic landscape design patterned after the work of Olmsted and Vaux, the tract had the initial advantage of picturesque rolling terrain with the Schuylkill River winding through its midst. Development since the mid-nineteenth century has been kept to a judicious minimum. The huge 1876 Centennial Exposition, which was located on the western side of the park, was almost entirely a temporary transformation, with the few permanent structures well integrated into the environs. Regrettably, recent years have seen the demolition of two of these, Horticultural Hall and the British Buildings, but Memorial Hall has been carefully fitted to contemporary uses. Other Victorian adornments include the Zoological Gardens, the rowing clubs' boathouses, and an ubiquituous series of Stick Style guardhouses.

In the late nineteenth century the riverside promenades became major boulevards out of the city, eventually connected to its heart by the Benjamin Franklin Parkway. These, too, were skillfully tailored so as not to interrupt the character of the land and still exist as two of the most impressive approaches into any city. The 1950s saw a decidedly unfortunate intrusion with the Schuylkill Expressway (recently widened), which takes little advantage of its magnificent route.

A major extension of the park lies along the Wissahickon Creek. Protecting a small, winding, wooded valley, this sector has been kept in a savage state that surpasses most expectations. The lower third of the Wissahickon Drive is open to cars and, while hazardous, is well worth the risk. Above the site of the old Rittenhouse Mills the park is a retreat that differs only slightly from its appearance two centuries ago (see Germantown).

**Fairmount
Park**

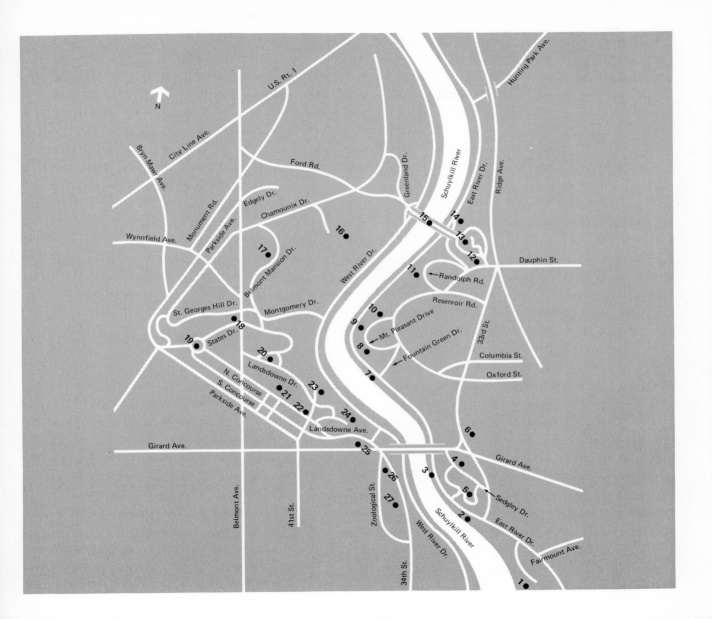

FP

1
Fairmount
Waterworks

1812-1822, Frederick Graff; later additions and alterations
Schuylkill River below Fairmount Avenue

A picturesque classical group, it replaced Latrobe's earlier facilities on Centre Square and formed the nucleus for the park's development.

2
Boathouse Row

East River Drive

2 A
Fairmount
Rowing
Association

Ca. 1870, 1900; addition 1903, Walter Smedley

2 B
Pennsylvania
Barge Club

Ca. 1900
Now U.S. Rowing Society

2 C
Crescent
Barge Club

1871; 1890, Charles Balderston

2 D
Bachelors
Barge Club

1893, Hazelhurst & Huckel

2 E
University
Barge Club

1871,1893

2 F Vesper and Malta Boat Clubs	1869; additions to Vesper 1898; additions to Malta 1880; 1901, G. W. & W. D. Hewitt
2 G College Boat Club	1873; later additions
2 H West Philadelphia Boat Club	Ca. 1873; alterations 1883, The Wilson Brothers Now Pennsylvania A. C. Rowing Association
2 I Undine Barge Club	1882, Furness & Evans
2 J Philadelphia Girls Rowing Club	Ca. 1869
2 K Sedgeley Club	1903, Arthur Brokie, built around an early nineteenth-century lighthouse

Boathouse Row has become a unique remnant of nineteenth-century summer architecture. Unfortunately the group is experiencing a slow decay coupled with gradual marring by unsympathetic additions.

3 Samuel Memorial

General scheme and middle terrace 1933, south terrace 1942, Paul Cret; north terrace 1957, Harbeson, Hough, Livingston & Larson
East River Drive below Girard Avenue

A series of formal sculpture gardens rendered in a sensitive manner similar to Rittenhouse Square (CC VI 18) and Logan Circle (CC VII 6), the detailing as well as the eclectic assemblage of sculpture displays the progression of Cret and his successors from the Beaux Arts to the modernistic.

4 Sedgley Porter's Lodge

1799, Benjamin Latrobe; alterations and additions ca. 1865
Sedgley Drive below Girard Avenue

Thought to be a vestige of the pioneer Gothick house long gone; details remain under Victorian additions.

FP

5
Lemon Hill,
Henry Pratt
House

Ca. 1800
Above Sedgley Drive
Open to the public

A splendid Federal country house that in many ways recalls a number of places Bulfinch designed outside of Boston. It rests on the same site as Robert Morris's The Hills, but it is not known exactly when it was built or what, if any, similarities it had to its predecessor.

6
Hatfield House

Ca. 1760; extensive additions and alterations ca. 1835; moved from Hunting Park Avenue 1930
Girard Avenue and 33rd Street

7
Group
of Angels

1972, Carl Milles, sculptor
East River Drive near Fountain Green Road

An effective informal grouping by Bower & Fradley, this is the latest of a large number of sculptural groups and pieces by major artists, in both romantic and formal settings, throughout the Park.

8
Mount Pleasant,
John McPherson
House

1761
Mt. Pleasant Drive
Open to the public

Cited by John Adams as "the most elegant country seat in Pennsylvania," it is the prime example of Georgian country places erected by prominent Philadelphians. These houses were often more elaborate than their owner's houses in the city. They also differed stylistically and in construction methods from the numerous simple houses that were built by the farmers throughout the region.

9
Rockland,
George Thompson
House

Ca. 1800
Mt. Pleasant Drive

10
Ormiston,
Edward Burd
House

1798
Reservoir Road

11
Laurel Hill,
Joseph Shute
House

Ca. 1748-1760; additions ca. 1800
Randolph Road

Laurel Hill illustrates that size was not necessarily a determining factor in a country seat, for while it was smaller than a number of contemporary farmhouses, it clearly was not one.

12
Woodford,
William Coleman
House

Ca. 1735; 1756; second story added
1772 for David Franks; later additions
Off 33rd and Dauphin Streets
Open to the public

The original house comprises what is
still the front but was of only one story.
There were other eighteenth-century
places of this nature around Philadelphia such as the Kinsey-Pemberton
"plantation" in South Philadelphia or
the simpler Fairhill built by Isaac Norris
in 1717, but all have long been demolished. The rear wing was not part of the
older house but the product of several
additions.

13
Summerville
(The Strawberry
Mansion),
William Lewis
House

1797; wings added 1825-1828 for
Joseph Hemphill
Off 33rd and Dauphin Streets
Open to the public

Built on the site of Charles Thomson's
Somerton (1774), the Georgian portion
of the Strawberry Mansion became an
unusual "center" for the carefully related Greek Revival additions.

14
Gateway
from the
Centennial
Exposition

1876, attributed to Frank Furness
East River Drive, north of Strawberry
Mansion Bridge

15
The Trolley
(Strawberry
Mansion)
Bridge

Ca. 1895, Samuel Smedley, engineer

The majority of the bridges in Fairmount Park have been harmonious additions. The lightness of this one's simple, direct expression makes it one of the finest.

16
Ridgeland

Ca. 1790-1810
Off Chamounix Drive

17
Belmont,
Richard Peters
House

Ca. 1730; 1743; 1745; 1755; 1762;
third-story added in the nineteenth
century
Belmont Mansion Drive

The much altered house now functions as a pleasant restaurant where a memorable view of center city as well as much of the park can be had.

FP

18
Ohio Building

1876, Heard & Sons (Cleveland)
Belmont Avenue and States Drive

A curious and rather charming display of native (Ohio) stone, it lends evidence that Furness was not alone in some of his approaches to design.

19
Catholic
Total Abstinence
Fountain

1876, Herman Kern, sculptor
North Concourse and States Drive

The Centennial Exposition was a veritable garden of High Victorian sculpture, better remembered for its sentimental evocations than as a creative expression in stone. This large ensemble was intended as an alternative to the beer garden.

20
Japanese
Exhibition
House

1953, Junzo Yoshimura (Tokyo), garden by Tansai Sano
Lansdowne Drive, east of Belmont Avenue
Open to the public

Made in Nagoya in 1953, exhibited at the Museum of Modern Art, and moved to Philadelphia in 1957, this unexpected feature of the park is closely patterned after Japanese prototypes of the sixteenth and seventeenth centuries.

21
Memorial Hall

1875, Herman Schwarzmann; altered
North Concourse at 42nd Street

When erected as the art museum for the Centennial Exposition, it far surpassed in size the few buildings in the country that were similarly used. Its architect had neither designed a building nor been subject to professional training before he built this and the other major halls for the event.

22
Richard Smith
Memorial
Gateway

1897-1912, John T. and James H. Windrim (James Windrim & Son); Daniel Chester French and Edward Potter, principal sculptors
North Concourse at 41st Street

23
Cedar Grove,
Joseph Paschall
House

1730s; 1752; additions for Isaac Wistar Morris between 1791-1799; moved from Frankford 1927
Cedar Grove Extension
Open to the public

Cedar Grove was built as a farmhouse and as such is distinguished from the majority of the other houses in the park. Morris doubled the house in the 1790s for use as a country place, however, so that while these additions were not out of keeping with the older sections, the final result is not really typical of farm-houses in the region.

24
Sweetbriar,
Samuel Breck
House

1797
Sweetbriar Extension
Open to the public

The understated elegance found particularly on the interior is perhaps more in character with Philadelphia than Lemon Hill (see FP I 5). While many of the elements are clearly carried over from the Georgian, the predominating simplicity marks it as of the Federal period.

25
Letitia Court
House

1713; moved from Letitia Court 1883; dormer added after 1894
Off Girard Avenue above 34th Street

One of the earliest surviving Philadelphia houses, it was moved and venerated in the mistaken belief than Penn once occupied it.

26
Philadelphia
Zoological
Gardens,
Entrance
Pavilions

1875, Furness & Hewitt; altered
Girard Avenue at 34th Street

Furness and Hewitt were the architects of many of the original buildings in this, the first American zoo. Hewitt's Antelope House (1877) is the only other piece of their work that remains. Theophilus Chandler's Bear Pits are still there as well. Some of the later pavilions were done by Paul Cret and Mellor & Meigs.

27
The Solitude,
John Penn
House

1785, Joseph H. Anderson (Maryland)
East side of zoo grounds

**North
Philadelphia**

The seemingly endless blocks of row houses that comprise much of North Philadelphia occupy land first conceived of as part of the Liberty lands—the agrarian focus for Penn's "Country Towne." The only acreage that even vaguely resembles the original intent is Fairmount Park. Early in the city's history dense urban development spread into the land above Vine Street, and soon communities such as Northern Liberties were formed in what was to have remained open country. By the early nineteenth century there was little to distinguish these streets from those in the older sections of town. Until the mid-1960s a sizable portion of the earlier handsome Georgian buildings was still extant, albeit in bad condition. All but a very few have now been leveled to make room for new industrial structures and Interstate 95. There have been no restoration efforts and surprisingly little documentation of these districts that contained a considerable portion of the city's early heritage.

Urban development continued at a rapid pace through to the early decades of this century. A large share of the city's factories were erected throughout the area, many concentrated along the Pennsylvania and Reading Railroad lines. The thousands of orderly, simple workers' houses were built in patterns of neighborhoods: factory, house, church, and store all closely integrated. Several streets such as the eastern portion of Girard Avenue developed as principal commercial centers. In the blocks immediately east of Broad Street, development took on a more middle-class character of plain but spacious row houses. Over the years these deteriorated into slums and have been subject to wholesale clearance for public housing, return to residential use in the pattern of the Greater Northeast, and for the expansion of the Temple University campus.

To the west of Broad Street the newly rich industrialists erected large, ostentatious piles during the latter part of the nineteenth century. If vulgar, some are nevertheless among the most interesting remains of the High Victorian era in the

city. But even at its height this was never a particularly fashionable area, and
by the turn of the century many of the
wealthiest had evacuated to the more
established areas. Today most of these
blocks have degenerated into slums of
the worst sort. The idyllic campus of
Girard College, which was later sur-
rounded by this gridiron development,
now provides poignant contrast.

  North Broad Street runs the length of
North Philadelphia, providing a great
boulevard down which one can get a
dramatic distant view of the center of
the city. The northern districts were the
last to be developed, with areas around
Olney Avenue dating from well into
this century. Primarily residential in
character, their treelined streets, flanked
by small row houses with large colo-
nialized porches, form much of the real
"Philly" part of town. Increasing urban
blight has made many forget that this is
a very large portion of the city, and
these clean and respectable neighborhoods are not to be discounted as unde-
sirable. Their appeal will perhaps be
realized once more as the suburban ideal
wears increasingly thin.

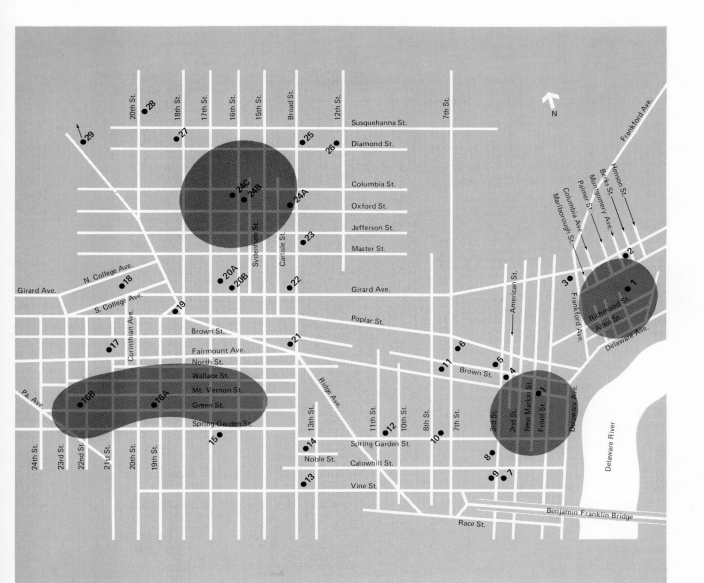

NP I

1
Northern Liberties and Fishtown

The area roughly bounded by Spring Garden and Laurel Streets, American to Front, has many houses that appear to date from the mid-eighteenth century in addition to a few handsome mercantile lofts of some hundred years later. Buildings between and along North Second and New Market Streets, Fairmount to Poplar, are particularly interesting. This portion of North Second Street contains an open square that was once a marketplace in complementary position to the one restored in Society Hill (see CC II 19 A). Unless an effective preservation effort is launched, there can be little hope that these buildings will survive long after Interstate 95 is completed and this forgotten area becomes "prime land."

Just to the northeast is a newer but interesting area known as Fishtown, roughly bounded by Delaware and Frankford Avenues and Hewson Street, which is still primarily residential. It gives a rather accurate picture of what most older sections of the city resembled for generations. A number of houses support splendidly inappropriate "improvements" dating from the 1940s in the form of aluminum fasciae, of a type usually reserved for diners, around their windows and doors.

2
First Presbyterian Church of Kensington

1857, Samuel Sloan; spire removed
418 East Girard Avenue

3
Kensington
National Bank

1877, Frank Furness
Girard and Frankford Avenues
Now First Pennsylvania Bank

4
Saint John's
Church

Ante 1818; several later alterations
American and Brown Streets
Now Romanian Orthodox Church

Probably a unique survival of a Neo-Classic motif that was never widely used in this country, the building remains architecturally significant despite the extensive alterations.

5
Odd Fellows'
Hall

1847, probably style of John Haviland
3rd and Brown Streets, NW corner
Now a warehouse

The sad state of decay of this structure makes eventual demolition more likely than rehabilitation.

6
Second
Dutch Reformed
Church

Ca. 1850; alterations 1919, 1966
811 North 7th Street
Now Saint Nicholas Russian Orthodox Church

7
Loft

Ca. 1860, attributed to Joseph Hoxie
333 North 3rd Street

An extraordinarily vivacious expression of Italianate forms is found in this brownstone loft, displaying some of the more flamboyant characteristic associated with the architect's work.

8
Alexander
Belting Company
Building

1916 et seq., Purcell & Elmslie (Chicago)
414 North 3rd Street

The only significant traces of the architects' style can be found in the offices on the seventh floor.

9
Horace
Potts & Co.
Warehouse

1896, Frank Miles Day & Brother
316-320 North Third Street

10
Friends
Guild House
Apartments

1964, Venturi & Rauch with Cope & Lippincott
711 Spring Garden Street

Although clearly related to Venturi's aesthetic credo, the awkward solemnity and plainness that have characterized much of his work also evoke recollection of anonymous early Quaker building of the region.

11
Friends
Housing
Co-Operation

1950, Oskar Stonorov
Franklin and 8th Streets, between Fairmount and Brown Streets

The first occasion in the country where a group of old houses was rehabilitated for low income families in renewal efforts, it was part of a large and mostly unrealized scheme for the area drawn up for the city by Louis Kahn. The concept of preserving neighborhoods as entities was integral to both Kahn's and Stonorov's philosophies and has been more apparent in Philadelphia's planning than in many American cities.

NP I

12
Edwin Schoettle
Company
Factory

1916, Day & Klauder
533 North 11th Street

An unusual venture for Day, it shows
competence in working with the simple
expression called for in design of a factory. Compare with the picturesque
Potts Warehouse (NP I 9).

13
Packard
Motor Car
Building

1910, Albert Kahn (Detroit); show-
rooms remodeled 1927, Philip Tyre;
altered
321 North Broad Street

14
Lasher Printing
Company
Building

1927, Philip Tyre
1309 Noble Street

Tyre, whose work is mostly forgotten,
proved to be an imaginative manipula-
tor of period design in industrial and
commercial buildings. The concrete bal-
conies here are particularly handsome.

15
United States
Mint

1898, William Aiken and James Taylor
(Washington, D.C.)
16th and Spring Garden Streets
Now Philadelphia Community College

16
Spring Garden District

16 A
J. J. Morton House

Alterations, additions, and front 1880, The Wilson Brothers
1901 Green Street

16 B
Kemble House

Ca. 1885, probably James H. Windrim; carriage house 1889, James H. Windrim
2201 Green Street

The 1500-2300 blocks of Green Street and adjacent streets are lined with an impressive assemblage of houses covering a broad spectrum of mid- and late-nineteenth-century design. By 1900 it was considered one of the most desirable areas in North Philadelphia, although the exodus to the suburbs by the wealthier residents began shortly thereafter. It has now long been in a state of the worst neglect, and of late a number of houses have seen demolition.

Most of these blocks are lined with brick houses in a simplified form of the Greek Revival built extensively throughout the city. This approach changed little over the years in North Philadelphia, save for a few concessions to popular taste such as mansard roofs and arched windows and doorways. The 2000 block of Brandywine Street is a very well maintained example of the smaller variety of this type house. The blocks to the north of Green Street—Mt. Vernon, Wallace, and North Streets—consist almost entirely of this more humble version. Those on the 2100 and 2200 blocks of Mt. Vernon Street have been fashionably restored. Houses on Green Street such as 1800-1806 are considerably more elaborate, but in dilapidated state. Other especially fine rows are 1701-1707 Wallace Street and a somewhat later variety found on the 2000 block of the same street.

Brownstone was not used widely in the area. A very notable example is the Wilson Brothers' Morton House. Of equal importance is 2201 Green, whose history is still unclear, but which is certainly one of the finest freestanding houses of its era remaining in the city.

2207 and 2209, while smaller, express an eagerness to compete. Many of the other Brownstones on Green Street are bedecked in Eastlake fashion, including 1810-1814, 2016-2018, and 2220. 1919 has the simple rectilinearity characteristic of much of Furness's work. Of the same era is Stephen Button's Spring Garden Lutheran Church (ca. 1859; altered) at 1520 Green.

2223 Green, attributed to The Wilson Brothers, is a wonderfully frantic expression of polychromy used to accentuate the rectilinearity common to design in the city at that time. 1533

Green, in the style of Willis Hale, and 2301 Green by Hale, are typical of another equally common and far less disciplined variety of High Victorian design in the area. 2144-2146 may well have been designed by Hazelhurst & Huckel (who were the architects for 2110, 2113, and 2112-2114) here working in a manner derived from Eyre and Day but lacking their restraint and grace.

The same blocks of Spring Garden Street are also worth noting for the multitude of early High Victorian row houses of considerable pretension that still exist, although the street has been more subject to the numerous changes that continually evolve along a major thoroughfare.

Rehabilitation efforts have not been numerous and have been executed with mixed results. 2009-2011 and 2113 Green are extremely sensitive though not elaborate rehabilitations, while work on the 1700 block of Mt. Vernon Street has been accomplished at considerable expense to the character of the houses.

If only a few of these houses could be justifiably deemed important pieces of architecture, the blocks as a whole are of considerable interest, providing a useful insight into the period, and they form an invaluable asset to the city.

17
Eastern State Penitentiary

1823-1836, John Haviland; altered
21st and Fairmount Avenue

The use of a radial plan and somber
Gothic mode made this building a prototype for a century of penal design.
Haviland was probably best known for
his prisons that were built throughout
the eastern United States.

18
**Girard College:
Founder's Hall
and Dormitories**

1833-1847, Thomas U. Walter
Girard and Corinthian Avenues

Founder's Hall is one of the most sublime, though least practical, monuments
in the Greek Revival; the dormitories
worked better but are strictly subsid-
iaries in the scheme. The Windrims did
much of the later work at the college,
some in Gothic.

NP I

___
19
Ridge Avenue
Farmers Market

1875, Davis Supplee
1820 Ridge Avenue

The market hall had experienced virtually no change until several years ago
when a notable and ruefully unsuccess-
ful venture of a Black business coopera-
tive induced minor alterations. At present the fate of one of the city's great
spaces appears to be less than promising.
Supplee is one of several Furness contemporaries whose work bears further
investigation.

___
20
Catholic
Complex

20 A
Church
of the Gesù

1879-1888, Edwin Durang
17th and Stiles Streets

20 B
Saint Joseph's
Preparatory
School

1968, Nolen, Swinburne & Associates
Girard Avenue and 16th Street

Durang was responsible for a sizable
portion of the large, often grotesque,
churches built in sections of the city
that grew after the Civil War. The Gesù
is perhaps his finest, most restrained
work, with a Baroque interior that has
few rivals in the country.

21
Central
Presbyterian
Church

1877, Collins & Autenreith
714 North Broad Street
Now Our Lady of the Blessed
Sacrament Church

22
Peter A. B.
Widener
House

1887, ca. 1895, Willis Hale; interiors,
George Herzog
Broad Street and Girard Avenue
Now Conwell Theological Seminary

This orgiastic assemblage of High Victorian eclecticism seems an appropriate
culmination to Hale's extensive residential work in the area (see NP I 24 and
29).

23
William Penn
High School

1968-1974, Mitchell/Guirgola
Associates
Broad Street, between Master and
Jefferson Streets

24 A
Alfred Burk
House

1909, Simon & Bassett
1500 Broad Street

24 B
House

1892
1517 North 16th Street

24 C
House

Ca. 1865
1530 North 16th Street

Many of the largest of the individual
houses are on North Broad Street.
1347 was built for actor Edwin Forrest
in 1855, richly detailed in late Italianate
dressing with an enormous addition.
1430 is one of the very few Richard-
sonian Romanesque houses in the city,
faithful in detail and massing until the
roof line, where proportion is splendidly abandoned. 1432 and 1438 are
good Second Empire Brownstone dwellings. As was the case here, rather than

building a house in the middle of two properties, a number of these dwellings were constructed in conventional row house form on one of the lots, the second left open as a side yard to it. These and the row at 1620-1636, if not by Sloan, are very close to known work that he did. The 2000 and 2100 blocks are lined with later Brownstones rich in Eastlake and other contemporary garnishes.

The 1500 and 1600 blocks of North 15th Street are comprised of rows of restrained Second Empire brick dwellings of dignified proportions. 1517 is perhaps the most elaborate, supporting a side yard and faced in brick. Likewise 1487 is a grand remodeling; the stable to its rear at 1432 Carlisle Street might be attributed to Frank Furness. 1417 Jefferson Street was erected in 1897 by Keen & Mead, closely following Eyre's precedent.

The 1500 block of North 16th Street is perhaps the most impressive of any in North Philadelphia. The front of 1517 is in a delicate, well-composed Renaissance, popularized by Stanford White and locally developed by Cope & Stewardson and Frank Miles Day, among others. The south side, however, is in a free Romanesque Revival and is certainly the finest example of this variety of creative eclecticism in the city. 1530 North 16th was probably erected in the 1860s. Its huge scale, assertively and flamboyantly detailed, marks it as a prime example of the more opulent aspects of the era. The 1600 block, in contrast, is rather plain, consisting entirely of rows austerely articulated in brick. 1614 is a lovely exception, similar to the Wilson Brothers' design at 2223 Green Street (see NP I 16).

1500-1526 North 17th Street and 1513-1533 Bouvier are a particularly ambitious group by Willis Hale (1886) while 1701-1707 Oxford are also clearly in his style. The church at Oxford and Sydenham, built in 1889, is an agreeable Queen Anne Revival work.

27
Church
of the
Advocate

1887-1897, Charles M. Burns, Jr.
18th and Diamond Streets

28
Women's
Homeopathic
Hospital

1884, Eyre & Jackson
20th Street above Susquehanna Avenue
Now Philadelphia Osteopathic Hospital

Designed more like an oversized Queen
Anne country house, it nonetheless reflects Eyre's attention to detail.

25
Bethlehem
Presbyterian
Church

1889, Theophilus Chandler
Broad and Diamond Streets

26
Free Church
of the
Annunciation

1883, Charles M. Burns, Jr.
12th and Diamond Streets

A charming and sensitive use of Romanesque forms in a small parish church
now isolated amidst renewal.

29
Speculative
Row Houses

1880-1885, Willis Hale
2301-2349 Thompson Street, 1900
block of 23rd Street and Judson Place

Representative of a number of row
houses designed by Hale in this section
where Messrs. Widener and Elkins were
among the principal developers. Hale
appears to have had a primary influence
on the design of much of the speculative
work in both North and West Philadelphia (see WP I 33 and WP I 36).

North
Philadelphia II

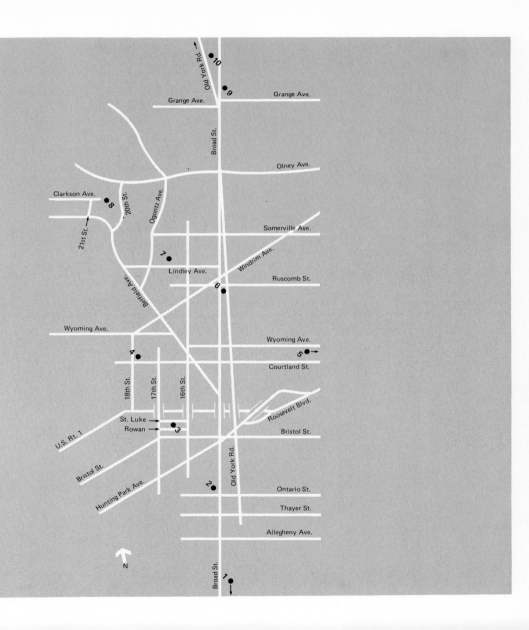

1

Philadelphia Saving Fund Society, Lehigh Branch

1924, Mellor, Meigs & Howe
Lehigh Avenue at 11th Street, NE corner

Work for this bank comprised the majority of the firm's nonresidential commissions. A twin to this distinguished abstraction of Renaissance design is in South Philadelphia at Broad and McKean Streets.

2

Temple University: Medical Research Building (1963) and Student Teaching Building (1967)

Nolen, Swinburne & Associates
Broad Street, west side, above Ontario Street

3

Houses for a Moravian Community

1885-1889, William Shaw, builder
1600 block St. Paul and Rowan Streets and adjoining section of 16th Street

Part of a four-block development around the Grace Moravian Church (demolished with the remaining houses), they are of a robust Queen Anne Revival style common in Philadelphia. Rowan Street is a mall.

5
**Wyoming Bank
and Trust
Company**

1924, McLanahan & Bencker
5th Street and Wyoming Avenue, SW
corner
Now Central-Penn National Bank

A haunting, awkward acknowledgment
of the substantial qualities expected of
a bank played against an expression of
lightness. A similar work by the firm for
the Oak Lane Trust Company at Broad
Street, Old York Road and 67th Avenue
survives.

4
**Stenton,
James Logan
House**

1728-1734; porch added 1754
18th Street and Courtland Avenue
Open to the public

Built for William Penn's secretary, Stenton is a primary example of Queen Anne
architecture in this country. It was one
of the earlier great country houses built
outside the city, although it gives only
faint indication of the elaborately detailed Georgian houses that were to
follow.

6
Philadelphia
Saving Fund
Society,
Logan Branch

1926, Mellor, Meigs & Howe
Broad and Ruscomb Streets

Howe's bank, in contrast to Bencker's Wyoming Bank and Trust Company, is still restrained and abstractly stylized but places full emphasis on the wall as solid mass. An identical branch is at 52nd and Ludlow Streets.

7
Wakefield,
Thomas Fisher
House

1798, Lindley Avenue and 16th Street
Now owned by the Colonial Dames of America

8
Belfield,
Nevie House

Ca. 1708; extensively enlarged ca. 1810 for Charles Willson Peale
2100 Clarkson Avenue

Remarkably the center of what was a large farm still exists, and combined with adjacent parks forms a pleasant remnant of country amid an otherwise densely developed area.

9
Dr. Bachrach's
Animal Hospital

1937, Silverman and Levy
5907 North Broad Street

10
Ahavath Israel
Synagogue

1935, Louis Kahn
6735 North 16th Street

The architect's first independent commission, in its modesty and directness,
was a departure from work he had been
doing in the offices of Paul Cret and
others.

**North
Philadelphia III**

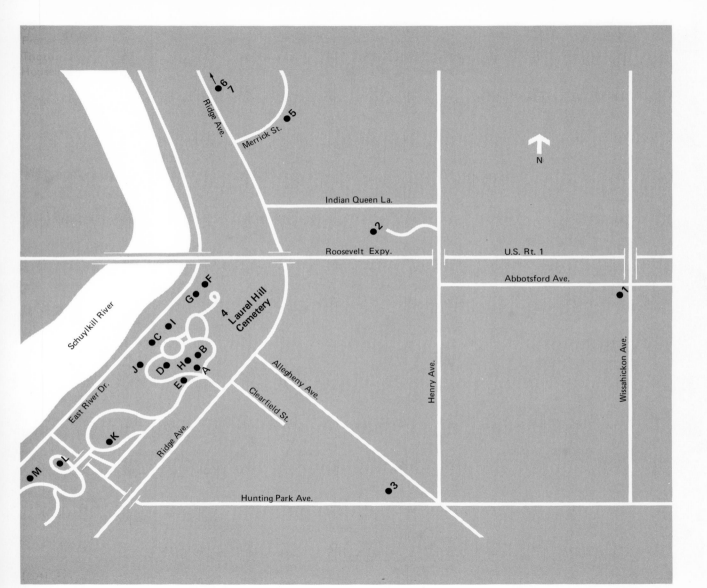

Ridge Ave.

6 7

5

Merrick St.

Indian Queen La.

2

Roosevelt Expy.

U.S. Rt. 1

Abbotsford Ave.

N

1

F

G

Laurel Hill
Cemetery

4

Schuylkill River

C I

Henry Ave.

Wissahickon Ave.

D H B

J

E A

Allegheny Ave.

East River Dr.

Clearfield St.

K

Ridge Ave.

L

M

3

Hunting Park Ave.

NP III

1
Atwater Kent Manufacturing Company Plant

1923 et seq., The Ballinger Company
Wissahickon Avenue and Abbottsford Road, SW corner

An early building that employed the "super span" saw-toothed skylight roof, designed and patented by Ballinger in 1920. Joining the peaks of the skylights with steel beams to form a transverse truss, the system eliminated the need for 60 percent of the supporting columns, thus opening large open spaces.

2
Women's Medical College, Ann Preston Building

1950, Roth & Fleisher, Thaddeus Longstreth, associate; additional floor 1955, Roth & Fleisher
Henry Avenue and Indian Queen Lane, SW corner
Now Medical College of Pennsylvania

A light airy building, well related to its site, it was one of the first postwar buildings in the city fully in the spirit of the International Style.

3
Church of Saint James the Less

1846, G. G. Place (of the Cambridge Camden Society), John E. Carver, supervising architect; bell tower and mausoleum 1908, John T. Windrim
Clearfield Street and Hunting Park Avenue

The first church in America that was a product of the English Ecclesiologists, it was, in turn, enormously influential on ensuing rural eclesiastical work in this country.

4
Laurel Hill Cemetery

1836, John Notman
3822 Ridge Avenue

"Philadelphia's preeminent necropolis," Laurel Hill is the second oldest rural cemetery in the country, and with Grove Street in New Haven and Mount Auburn in Cambridge established a pattern for development which has seen little deviation since. One of the architect's first commissions, it was won in competition with entries from Strickland and Walter, among others. The grounds, situated on a choice piece of land overlooking the Schuylkill, are laid out in Romantic spirit and contain many extremely fine examples of period funerary sculpture. A Gothic chapel designed by Notman and other buildings on the premises have long been demolished, but his entrance gate and offices remain.

A number of monuments that he did for individuals have also been identified.

Unfortunately, no comprehensive study has been done on the cemetery, and only a small number of the most interesting tombs can be listed.

NP III

4 A
Housing for
Old Mortality

(above main entrance)
Ca. 1840, John Notman

4 B
Alfred Miller
Monument

(Section A, lots 68-69)
1840, William Strickland

4 C
Joseph S. Lewis
Monument

(Section H, lots 6-9)
1838, John Notman

4 D
John and
Margaret Evans
Tomb

(Section A, lots 1-4)
Between 1847 and 1852, John Notman

4 E
John Notman
Monument

(Section M, lot 165)
1870, probably not by John Notman

4 F
Robert Gratz
Tomb

(Section W, lots 309-310)
Ca. 1873

4 G
Captain
Stephen
Lavalette
Monument

(Section W, lots 122-124)
1860, John Notman

4 H
Charles Graff
Tomb

(Section B, lots 96-99)
Between 1846 and 1865, John Notman

4 I
Esther Ball
Tomb

(Section G, lots 110-112)
1863, Thomas U. Walter

4 J
Henry Charles
Lea
Monument

(Section S, lot 36)
1909, Zantzinger & Borie (Alexander S.
Calder, sculptor)

4 K
Berwind
Monument

(Section 15, lot 39)
1882, D. Kornbau

4 L
William Mullen
Monument

(Section U, lot 562)
1933, Presbrey-Leland Studios (New
York City)

4 M
Sarah Harrison
Tomb

(Section 9, lot 72)
1850, John Notman

5
Schuylkill
Falls
Public Housing

1955, Oskar Stonorov
Ridge Avenue and Merrick Street

The apartment blocks maintain a complementary tension with the terrain giving them considerable visual strength even when viewed from a distance. As low-income housing, they invite an ironic comparison with their "luxury" neighbors across the river.

6
Wissahickon
Station,
Reading
Railroad

Ca. 1883, probably Furness & Evans; parts removed
Ridge Avenue and Reading Railroad

This is probably one of the one hundred and twenty-five buildings that Furness's office is known to have designed for the Reading between 1879 and 1884 but for which no specific documentation has yet been found.

7
Manayunk

The rugged and varied topography of this early nineteenth-century industrial town gives it a particular character worth exploring. While there is little of individual architectural note, the steep, often winding cobblestoned streets lined with stark workers' dwellings provide a very human setting. Most buildings are simple, indigenous variations of the Federal rows in Center City. Others, equally plain, built in the late Victorian era, hint at Eastlake and Furness influences. Many of the handsome mills along the canal and Schuylkill River are still used.

The
Northeast

Much of the lower section of the North-east, sprawling over former farmlands, is visually indistinguishable from adjacent neighborhoods in North Philadelphia and, like them, represents a mixture of industrial and related residential uses. Old communities such as Frankford retain much of their character but have recently lost their important landmarks, including Port Royal and Chalkley Hall. Under the Elevated along Kensington and Frankford Avenues, a lively and con-gested commercial center continues to thrive. Farther up the Delaware, Holmesburg is an interesting but dis-tinctly less urban community. Keeping its nineteenth-century scale and a num-ber of older dwellings. Fox Chase and Bustleton retain elements of their early crossroads town structure.

The intensive development of the Northeast came after the Second World War, with a mass exodus from older sec-tions of the city by the white lower-middle class, and has slowed down little since. The new settlements main-tain the tradition-oriented status of neighborhood solidarity found in the communities left behind. Development has continued in row-house patterns, and even when units are semidetached

they retain the basic row character of older sections of the city. If it is tempt-ing to muse over their fake stone fronts and absurd ventures into the world of ornament, it is the lack of creative or re-ally comprehensive planning more than the buildings themselves which marks the ultimate failure of the Northeast as anything save a temporary escape from some of the uglier problems of city existence. The speculation continues at a rampant pace and will inevitably con-sume a large portion of Bucks and Mont-gomery Counties.

Open space is now a rarity. The Penny-pack Creek Valley was fortunately spared some years ago and incorporated into the Fairmount Park system. The Roosevelt Boulevard was another green-belt, its ten traffic lanes divided by planted strips lined with trees in a grand Beaux Arts manner. Unfortunately in-creased usage has brought extensive re-construction in the most mediocre free-way style. Much of the new Interstate 95 is elevated and allows the motorist to overlook the area in a matter of minutes.

The
Northeast I

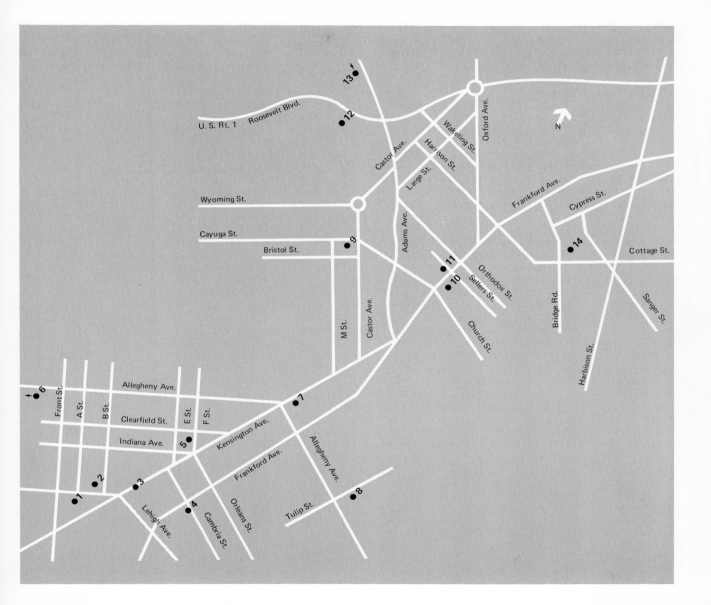

NE I

1
Episcopal
Hospital

1860-1874, Samuel Sloan (including the Memorial Church of Saint Luke the Good Physician); later buildings G. W. & W. D. Hewitt, and Cope & Stewardson; Tower Building 1933, Day & Zimmerman; recent work Vincent Kling & Associates.
Front Street and Lehigh Avenue

Based on the then best European principals of hospital design, Sloan's work placed wards in individual buildings connected by corridors for maximum therapeutic light and air and minimum contamination. A sense of the original complex remains quite distinguishable despite many later alterations and additions.

2
Bromley Mills

Ca. 1860
Lehigh Avenue and A Street

3
The Frankford
Elevated
Railroad

1915-1922, Department of City Transit, City of Philadelphia; station buildings William H. Lee
Front Street from Market Street to Kensington Avenue, Kensington Avenue to Frankford Avenue, Frankford Avenue to Bridge Street

An expedient part of a massive transit expansion program, its industrial frankness lends a certain vulgar intrigue as well as unity to the street level.

4
Trinity Presbyterian Church

1861-1876, Thomas W. Richards
Frankford Avenue and Cambria Street

5
Free Library of Philadelphia, McPherson Square Branch

1915, Wilson Eyre & McIlvaine
McPherson Square, Indiana Avenue and F Street

Eyre's approach to design remained very personal even when using a classical vocabulary. This quality is especially evident in comparison with the Lehigh Branch at 6th Street and Lehigh Avenue (G. W. & W. D. Hewitt 1906), which is a more standard version of the Carnegie Library.

6
North American Lace Company Factory

1903, William Steele & Sons, Co.
Glenwood and Allegheny Avenues at 8th Street

7
Midway Theatre

1932, Magaziner, Eberhart & Harris
Allegheny Avenue, below Kensington Avenue

The neighborhood commercial center at Kensington and Allegheny Avenues is one of the many erected throughout the city in the first half of the century which fulfill an important visual function as an identifiable "center" for a community. It is an element almost never present in recent developments. This group is one of a minority that has not been marred by gaudy commercial additions in later years. The theatre, which is quite simple on the exterior, has an auditorium that is one of the most eventful moderne fantasies remaining locally.

8
Northeastern Regional Hospital Additions

1966, Garner & White
Allegheny Avenue and Tulip Street

A low-budget tower, simply expressed, that adds a powerful focus to the neighborhood

9
Carl Mackley
Houses

1933, Alfred Kastner and Oskar
Stonorov, with W. Pope Barney
Castor Avenue, between Cayuga and
Bristol Streets

Sponsored by the American Federation
of Hosiery Workers, this project represents an initial and important merging of
housing patterns of the United States
with those of the Continent. Units,
domestic in character, are placed around
varying, green central courts but are also
given the visually orderly and purposeful
expression of the International Style.
Carefully planned to suit the needs of its
tenants, it has remained one of the more
successful efforts of its kind in the
country.

10
Frankford
Avenue First
Presbyterian
Church

1859, John McArthur, Jr.
Frankford Avenue and Church Street

McArthur was already breaking away
from the conventional Romantic modes
in which he had been practicing and here
displayed an inventive sensitivity to the
industrial orientation of the community.

11 **Saint Mark's** **Church**	1907, Watson & Huckel 4442 Frankford Avenue One of the better works of this firm of ecclesiastical heavies, its budget demanded a restraint that was handled with accomplished sophistication.
12 **Friends** **Hospital**	Adams Avenue and Roosevelt Boulevard
12 A **Main Building**	1814, et seq., Israel Maule, carpenter; mansard roof 1871, William Kees; later additions and alterations
12 B **Cope Building**	1888, Cope & Stewardson
12 C **Evans Memorial** **Building**	1891, Cope & Stewardson; porch removed; enlarged The first private institution exclusively devoted to treatment of the insane in the country. Freely patterned after the York Retreat in England, it was, in turn, the main antecedent for later asylum designs (WP I 38) leading to the Kirkbride type (see WP I 42). Cope & Stewardson's work reflects the experimentation in the firm's early years.
13 **Hill Creek** **Houses**	1936, Thomas & Martin, with William Antrim Adams and Rising Sun Avenues The city's first public housing project has, in many ways, remained one of its best. Well-scaled units are arranged in a seemingly informal manner around green open spaces that, in this case, lend themselves well to human use. Subsequent projects were larger and of a higher density but tended to follow more rigid patterns of organization and often failed to meet their inhabitants' needs as effectively. J. W. Johnson Houses (W. Pope Barney, 1939), Tasker Houses (Karcher and Ziegler, 1939), and Richard Allen Houses (Paul Cret, 1940) bear comparison.
14 **Mount Sinai** **Cemetery** **Mortuary Chapel**	1891, Furness, Evans & Company Bridge and Cottage Streets

**The
Northeast II**

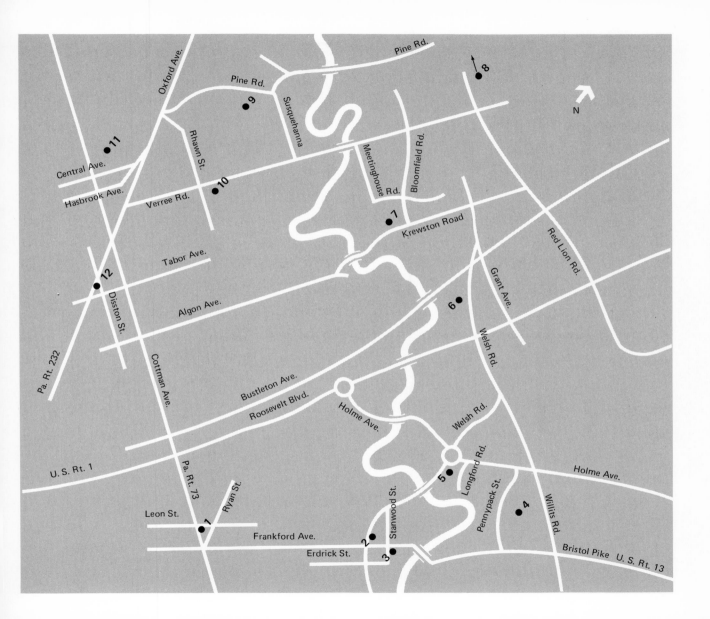

NE II

1
Mayfair Theatre

1936, David Supowitz
7300 Frankford Avenue

The usual flamboyance of the moderne
movie house was rare in Philadelphia.
This delightful exception by one of the
city's principal theater architects turns
its difficult site to an advantage, with
architecture and advertising sensibly
unified.

2
**Peter Rambo
(Rembrandt
Peale) House**

Ca. 1783, Peter Rambo, carpenter;
enlarged 1810 for William Griffith;
additions ca. 1857
8100 Frankford Avenue

The small community of Holmesburg
still boasts a number of pleasant early
nineteenth-century works along the old
coach road.

3
**Emmanuel
Episcopal
Church**

1857, Sloan & Stewart
8100 Frankford Avenue

**4
Pennypack
Woods
War Housing**

1942, Howe, Stonorov & Kahn; store and administration building 1944, Stonorov & Kahn
Willits Road and Pennypack Street, between Holme Avenue and Bristol Pike

Planning, more than architectural design, marks the ultimate value of the project. Buildings generally conform to the contours of the landscape, forming irregular and pleasant open spaces.

**5
Green Belt Knoll
Development**

1957, Montgomery & Bishop
Longford Road

Decidedly unusual for a contractor's development, the contrast with the majority of profiteering in the area is painfully evident.

**6
Saint Luke's
Church**

1860, Richard Upjohn & Son
1946 Welsh Road

Upjohn's gift for working creatively within his standard modes is well exemplified in this minor but attractive work.

7
Pennypack Baptist Church

1774, rebuilt 1805
Krewston Road below Bloomfield Road

8
Budd Company, Red Lion Plant

1942 et seq., The Ballinger Company, Roberts & Schaefer (New York), engineering associates
Red Lion Road above Bustleton Avenue

The Roberts & Schaefer developed "barrel shell" or "Z-D" type of roof construction was a fast and economical method ideally suited to wartime construction and used extensively during the 1940s. Its highly expressionistic qualities give a large plant such as this almost sublime monumentality.

9
Ury House

Ca. 1645; 1728; ca. 1790 by Miers Fisher; extensive additions and alterations 1841 for Stephen Crawford, altered
Pine Road above Strahle Street

Perhaps one of the oldest surviving structures in the city. It is now wrapped in a Regency "Grecian Villa" somewhat reminiscent of the residential commissions of John Haviland.

10
Knowlton,
William Rhawn
House

1880, Frank Furness
Verree Road and Rhawn Street, NE corner

Furness's rural domestic work was often derived from that of his teacher, Richard Morris Hunt. Here the forms of Hunt's Appleton House in Newport, Rhode Island (1875, demolished), are clearly echoed but given a robust cohesiveness with horizontal emphasis so often specific to Philadelphia design.

11
Burholme,
Joseph Ryerss
House

1857
Burholme Park, Cottman and Central Avenues
Open to the public

A magnificent Italianate villa with bursts of High Victorian exuberance. A number of similar endeavors once existed in the area.

12
Trinity Church

1711; wings 1833; tower 1839; minor additions 1932
Tabor Avenue and Disston Street, SE corner

**South
Philadelphia**

The northeastern corner of South Philadelphia is the oldest section of the city, first settled by the Swedes as Wicaco, and now a part of the district of Southwark. A healthy working-class community, it contained more prerevolutionary buildings than any other area in the city. While almost all of these structures had been altered, some to a considerable degree, the narrow streets and alleys, lined with what was still discernibly very old fabric, conjured a far more plausible image of the colonial era than does Society Hill. In 1968 a large portion of the district was removed for an elevated freeway. With the remaining blocks disintegrating, a massive preservation/restoration injection may ruefully be the only way it will survive.

Most of South Philadelphia contains modest developments of the late nineteenth and early twentieth centuries, with limited, often neighborhood, industry. Traditionally the settling place for each new immigration wave, it is still largely comprised of a physically indistinguishable quilt of ethnic communities. Such commercial developments as the Italian Market on South 9th Street and the once primarily Jewish concentration on South Street suggest the strong cohesive character that still keeps most of the area from deterioration. The recent threat of the Crosstown Expressway, which would have completely eliminated South Street, resulted in the noticeable decline in the street's prosperity. While the freeway plans fortunately have been shelved and there is considerable interest in rejuvenation, recovery has been slow.

Buildings of architectural interest in South Philadelphia are few. Broad Street, which runs the length of the area, is uniformly unexciting. A few flamboyant High Victorian houses and the former Ridgway Library are (and were) the only monuments to catch the eye.

To the east Thomas U. Walter's Philadelphia County (Moyamensing) Prison,
with its Egyptian Debtor's Wing
(1832 and 1836), was leveled in 1968
after abandonment, at the insistence of
the neighborhood. In general the houses
are unassuming, unadorned, solid, and
usually well maintained, not dissimilar
in style to those of the same period in
Baltimore. And South Philadelphia has
maintained its plainness. If prosaic to
the cultured eye, it is certainly agreeably
scaled, structured to the lives of the
inhabitants, and has an integrity that
few urban renewal projects can
approach.

  The southern end of South Philadelphia
delphia, once marshes and landfill, in
recent years has been developed in part
as a judiciously planned wholesale food
distribution center. Comparable acreage,
however, is parkland, the site of the 1926
Sesqui-Centennial. The neighborhood
has also now become a repository for
stadiums, including Skidmore, Owings
& Merrill's Spectrum.

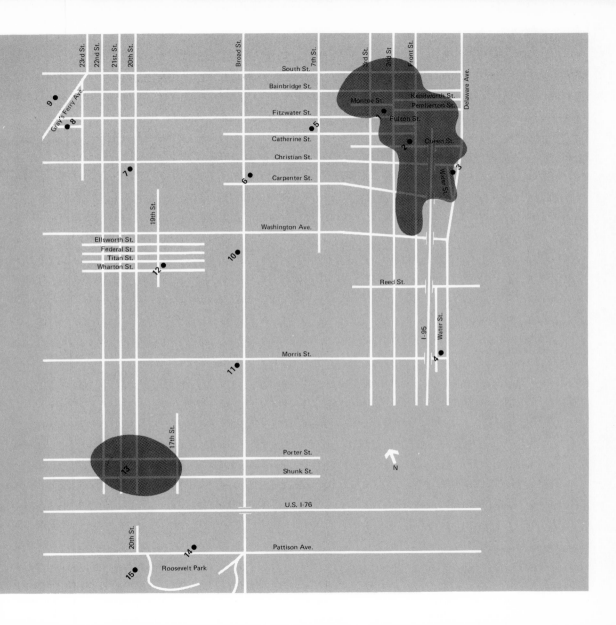

Southwark remains a significant representation of the working man's community of the eighteenth and early nineteenth centuries, containing a surprising variety of buildings. While the oldest, until the last decade it was only one of several such neighborhoods in the city. With urban renewal efforts, however, it has become virtually unique.

Front Street, from Lombard to Washington, contains a good cross section of the Georgian houses in the area. Bainbridge Street retains many of its more modest dwellings. The street becomes a large open square from the 300 to the 500 blocks. Kenilworth Street between Front and 2nd Streets has many of the finest examples of dwellings typical of the area. Monroe Street, from 2nd to 3rd Streets, has a concentration of recently restored and new houses that are the beginning of a speculative boom that promises to permeate the section.

Pemberton Street, from Front to 2nd Streets, is lined with Post-Georgian work of the early 1800s. At the Front Street end is Workman Place (1798-1810), which also incorporates houses from 742-752 Front Street (ca. 1754-1813) and the little houses dated 1748 built by George Mifflin. Restored by the Octavia Hill Association about 1906, these were the only residences consciously maintained along somewhat original lines. Immediately to the south is Fitzwater Street, perhaps the most interesting of the numerous alleys throughout the district. Streets farther south are also of note. Along Carpenter Street above Front Street is Sparks's Shot Tower (1808), which was the first of its type in the country and is now the focus for a playground.

2
Church of the
Redeemer
for Seamen and
Their Families
and
Charles Brewer
School

1878, Frank Furness
Front and Queen Streets, NW corner

3
Gloria Dei,
Old Swedes'
Church

1698, John Smart and John Buett, carpenters; wings 1703; tower 1733 (?); interior alterations 1845, Samuel Sloan
Water Street below Christian Street

A historical memento of the early Swedish settlers, the church formed a center for the small community now beyond the expressway.

4
J. T. Bailey
and Company
Factory

1882; additions 1885, 1889, style of Furness, Evans & Company; additions 1895, Furness, Evans & Company; tower removed and altered
Water and Morris Streets

5
Church of the
Evangelists

1886 (incorporating the tower of an 1823 church), Louis Baker and E. J. Dallett (of Furness, Evans & Co.); Saint Martin's School Building, 1906, Louis Baker; interior alterations after 1922 with conversion to the Samuel S. Fleisher Art Memorial.
719 Catherine Street
Open to the public (limited hours)

The former church has become a fascinating repository of artifacts dominated by the fin de siècle murals of Violet Oakley and Nicola D'Ascenzo. Philadelphia in the first decades of this century was a center for noted artisans including Henry Mercer, Henry Lee Willet, and Samuel Yellin.

6
Ridgway
Library

1871-1877, Addison Hutton
Broad and Christian Streets

Great galleried spaces of High Victorian dimensions and exuberance are fronted with a Greek Revival facade as anachronistic in style as the building is in location. Its interior gutted and remodeled, it will now serve its community as a recreation center.

7
Church of
Saint Charles
Borromeo

1868-1876, tower completed 1904,
Edwin Durang
20th and Christian Streets

In both North and South Philadelphia one can see a striking contrast between the elaborate churches of the large Catholic congregations and the visually dull neighborhoods around them. Durang, inevitably inspired by LeBrun's use of the Baroque, was able to manipulate its forms with appropriate fervor.

8
Residential
Development

Blocks adjacent to Catherine Street, between 23rd and 24th Streets

8 A
Madison Square

Ca. 1869, Charles Leslie and Alexander Smith

8 B
Saint Alban's
Place

Ca. 1865, Charles Leslie

These blocks were an early use of landscaped walks in place of streets and enhance a quiet enclave of simple houses, typical of many in South Philadelphia.

SP

9
United States
Naval Asylum
(Naval Home)

1827-1833, William Strickland
Grays Ferry Avenue

Virtually unaltered, this is an important example of early institutional architecture. The domed assembly hall is a fine adaptation from contemporary work in England. Lanning Hall to the rear was designed by John McArthur, Jr. (1864-1868).

10
David Garrison
House

1884, Willis Hale
1164 South Broad Street
Now Saint Rita's Parish House

11
Civic Complex

Broad and Morris Streets, SW corner

11 A
Free Library
of Philadelphia,
Broad-Morris
Branch

1965, Nolen, Swinburne & Associates

11 B
District Health
Center No. 2

1965, Norman Rice

This quiet, inviting neighborhood focus was part of a planned program in the 1950s and early 1960s for the erection of good contemporary community civic structures throughout the city.

12
Church of the
Holy Comforter

1874, Furness & Hewitt; altered
19th and Titan Streets
Now 19th Street Baptist Church

13
Girard Estate

13 A
Gentilhommière,
Stephen Girard
House

Ca. 1750; ca. 1798
Girard Park, 21st and Porter Streets

13 B
Development
for the
Girard Estate

1909-1914, John T. and James H.
Windrim (James Windrim & Son)
17th to 22nd Streets, Porter to Shunk
Streets

Some 800 homes serviced by a shopping
center, library, power plant, and other
facilities comprise this project, which
is sensitively broken down to a pleasant,
humane scale, within the established
grid pattern.

14
United States
Naval Hospital

1929-1933, Karcher & Smith
Pattison Avenue and 16th Street

Zenith! . . . almost. Architects pursuing
the ultimate visions of Hugh Ferris and
John Vassos sometimes forgot. . . .

15
Bellaire

Original building ca. 1675 by Thomas
Jacobs, Jr.; main house probably built
ca. 1720 by Samuel Preston
Franklin D. Roosevelt Park, off Pattison
Avenue

This small house remains a significant
example of early Georgian design. The
woodwork on the interior is especially
handsome. The building erected by
Jacobs was most likely the adjacent
structure lying to the northwest.

**West
Philadelphia**

One of the city's first suburbs, early development came to West Philadelphia in the 1840s with the erection of a number of large romantic villas. Less elaborate, but attractive, speculation was concurrent, forming communities such as Powelton and what is now known as Spruce Hill. While the majority of the larger dwellings have been demolished (mostly by the University of Pennsylvania's expansion program), a good portion of the speculative work remains. Sadly, Powelton, which is perhaps the best concentration of these houses, stands threatened by further University City development.

The second half of the nineteenth century saw rapid residential growth, consisting almost entirely of row houses, built to meet the large exodus of the new middle class from older sections of the city. It is this development that forms the bulk of West Philadelphia. Many of the rows are splendid eccentric variations of Victorian bourgeois taste combined with Philadelphia regionalism in one of its least-enlightened moments. Lancaster Avenue is a major shopping area, besieged with a visual confusion which, if now degenerating, is potentially a strong attribute. Adjacent residential streets including Mantua Avenue are filled with scores of elaborate row houses that have decayed badly. But the largest number of buildings are simple, well-kept dwellings, resting on quiet,

often treelined streets. Kingsessing still retains a few eighteenth-century buildings but has long since lost any of the character of its earlier days.

The eastern end of West Philadelphia has been the site of most of the changes that have occurred over the last fifty years. The focus of activity has been the University of Pennsylvania, whose recent wave of expansion has provided the city with a large and interesting eclectic campus in brick. Spreading from a core, much of which was designed by Cope & Stewardson, additions include some notable buildings by Kahn, Giurgola, and Geddes. The majority of the buildings are of pleasant if not always superb design with remarkably few visual disasters. Adjacent Drexel University, on the other hand, while more cohesive, is uniformly dismal. A new outgrowth of the two is the University City Science Center, which promises to line Market Street with inoffensive office buildings. The nearby civic center, erected over the span of a century, despite its size, is particularly unspectacular.

To the southwest a few individual remnants of Swedish and prerevolutionary English settlements still exist, but save for Bartram Park the accompanying rural environment has long since disappeared. The extensive lowlands and marshes to the south contain the ever-expanding International Airport, a wildlife refuge, and the city's surviving fort.

West
Philadelphia I

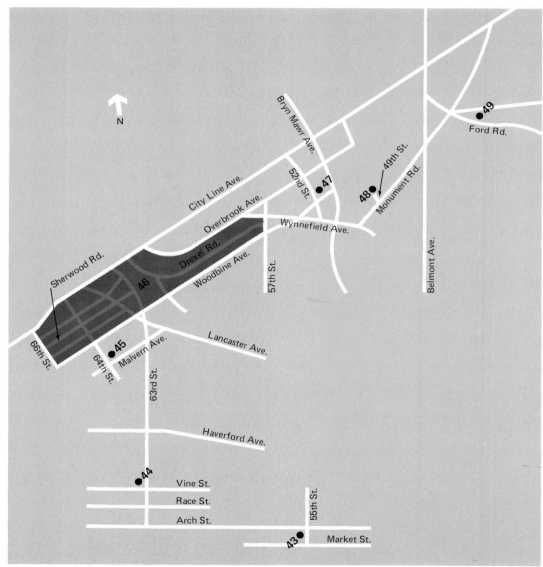

N

Bryn Mawr Ave.

52nd St.

City Line Ave.

Overbrook Ave.

Wynnefield Ave.

49th St.

Monument Rd.

Belmont Ave.

Ford Rd.

● 49

● 47

48 ●

Sherwood Rd.

Drexel Rd.

Woodbine Ave.

57th St.

46

● 45

64th St.

Malvern Ave.

Lancaster Ave.

63rd St.

66th St.

Haverford Ave.

● 44

Vine St.

Race St.

Arch St.

55th St.

43 ●

Market St.

Fairmount Ave.

Haverford Ave.

Lancaster Ave.

●41

Haverford Ave.

Spring Garden St.

●40

Hamilton St.

Baring St.

35th St.

36

Powelton Ave.

42nd St.

●42

Market St.

●39

●38

●37

35A

35B

Race St.

JFK Blvd.

●1

●2

49th St.

48th St.

46th St.

45th St.

44th St.

43rd St.

42nd St.

41st St.

40th St.

39th St.

38th St.

37th St.

34th St.

33rd St.

32nd St.

31st St.

30th St.

Chestnut St.

●25

●23

●16

●3

●4

Walnut St.

●32A

●30

●24

●22

●26

●7

●8B

●6

●8A

Locust St.

33

●32B

●27 ●28

●13

●5

Spruce St.

●31

●29

●21

●14

●9

Pine St.

●32C ●32D

●20 ●17

●15

●10 ●11

South St.

Baltimore Ave.

●32E

●18

Curie Ave.

Springfield Ave.

●34

●19

Woodland Ave.

University Ave.

●12

Schuylkill Expressway

Schuylkill River

N

WP I

**1
Pennsylvania
Railroad
Station
("30th
Street")**

1927-1933, Graham, Anderson, Probst
& White (Chicago)
30th Street and John F. Kennedy Boulevard

Despite its potential to impress, the
building's exterior lacks a distressing
portion of the needed vitality. Grouped
with the Post Office (1930) across Market Street, it helps create a strangely
barren, large-scaled entrance to West
Philadelphia. The interior is, however,
of a breed becoming rare, and if the
experience is not the same exhilaration
once rendered by the old Penn Station
in New York, there is still the feeling of
Having Arrived.

   The Steam Heating and Auxiliary
Power Plant by the station architects
as well as Paul Cret's Schuylkill River
railroad bridge (1927) are also noteworthy.

**2
Philadelphia
Bulletin
Building**

1953, Howe & Brown
31st and Market Streets

An appropriate complement to the railroad station, the series of escalators and
the neon-lit arcade comprise the principal features of interest.

**3
Centennial
National Bank**

1876, Frank Furness; alterations and one-story wing 1899, Frank Miles Day & Brother
32nd and Market Streets, SE corner
Now First Pennsylvania Bank

The bold forms around the entry recall later Furness banks now demolished. This too is threatened by Drexel Institute's tasteless expansion program.

**4
Drexel
Institute of
Technology**

1890, The Wilson Brothers
32nd and Chestnut Streets, NE corner

Beyond the heavy terracotta frosting lies a space of light.

WP I

University of
Pennsylvania

5
Class of 1923
Hockey Rink

1969, McMillan Associates (New York)
32nd and Walnut Streets, SE corner

6
Garage

1963, Mitchell/Giurgola Associates
32nd and Walnut Streets, NW corner

The simple and direct articulation forms an imposing utilitarian structure. The difference in the architects' approach between this and the later garage (WP I 11) bears comparison. Both function as visual gates to the university community.

7
Hill Hall

1960, Eero Saarinen & Associates (New Haven)
34th and Walnut Streets, NE corner

An enormous, skylit central court provides a surprising contrast to the pile's austere exterior and the cubicle-like rooms that comprise the bulk of it.

8
Moore School
of Engineering
Additions

Harold Pender Laboratories, 1958, Geddes, Brecher & Qualls; Graduate Research Center, 1967, Geddes, Brecher, Qualls & Cunningham
33rd and Walnut Streets, SW corner

The earlier addition is a notable exercise in economy, with the structure itself having a rich variety of surfaces.

9
Weightman Hall

1904, Frank Miles Day & Brother
33rd and Spruce Streets, NE corner

**10
Free Museum
of the
University of
Pennsylvania**

1893, west court 1899, west rotunda
1912, mid-section 1926, Wilson Eyre,
Jr., Frank Miles Day & Brother, and
Cope & Stewardson, associated architects; additions 1969, Mitchell/Giurgola
Associates
33rd and South Streets

There is little doubt that this may be
cited as the high point of Philadelphia's
Creative Eclecticism. Although a joint
effort, Eyre seems to have provided the
final design sophistication and detail,
creating a warm and artful horizontal
structure. Comparison with the contemporary Metropolitan Museum of Art in
New York emphasizes much of the
peculiar local character and strength.
Less than half of the original plan was
executed. Giurgola's recent addition,
while very much its own entity, comple-
ments its elder well and provides an
interesting union of two important
moments of Philadelphia design.

WP I
University of
Pennsylvania

11 **Garage**	1968, Mitchell/Giurgola Associates South Street and Convention Avenue, SW corner
12 **Michael Murphy** **Field House**	1939, Kenneth Day Lower playing fields, off University Avenue

13
Library

1888, 1914, Furness, Evans & Company;
addition 1923; addition 1931, Robert
McGoodwin
34th Street, between Walnut and Spruce
Streets
Now Furness Building

One of Furness's (and the city's) most
important buildings, its painfully asser-
tive articulation reaches noble proportions on the interior through a magnificent sequence of spaces where there is
an ever-present struggle between masonry and iron construction. The stacks

were to be expanded considerably as the library increased in size. They were, however, later capped by a rather unfortunate wing also designed by the firm. McGoodwin was going to coat the cake with an inoffensive Gothic icing, the better to match Trumbauer's Irvine Auditorium (1926), adjoining to the south.

14
College Hall

1871, Thomas W. Richards
Main Quadrangle

The result of a competition, this multi-purpose structure brought to the new campus what was then considered the ultimate in collegiate design. The pinnacles and towers that were once plentiful have unfortunately been removed. Nearby Logan Hall is also part of the original group.

15
Houston Hall

1895, Milton Medary and William Hays (of Frank Miles Day & Brother); additions 1933, Robert McGoodwin
Spruce Street above 34th Street

WP I

University of
Pennsylvania

**16
Law School**

1899, Cope & Stewardson; alterations
and additions to the complex, Carroll,
Grisdale & Van Alen, 1958-1968
34th and Chestnut Streets, SW corner

Even after their shift to working primarily in a Beaux Arts academicism,
Cope & Stewardson generally showed
more interest in pre-Renaissance styles
for precedent. While well rendered there
is nonetheless an uneasiness in the Georgian formality of this building.

**17
Men's
Dormitories**

1895-1901, Cope & Stewardson; south-
east quadrangle 1911, 1928, Stewardson
& Page; additions 1955-1960
Spruce Street, between 36th and 38th
Streets

Unlike either the firm's work at Bryn
Mawr College or English prototypes, the
dormitories here were of an urban scope
appropriate to their enormous size as
well as the new neighborhood scale.
Most of the scheme was realized; however, the absence of the great dining
hall, which was to complement the
Memorial Tower on the south side, is
noticeable. Built at a time when univer-
sities were beginning to be identified
with their own architectural styles, they
were instrumental in establishing the
character of the work done here (much
of it by the same firm) for almost half
a century.

18
Alfred Newton Richards Medical Research Building and Biology Building

1957-1964, Louis Kahn
Hamilton Walk, below 38th Street

Cited in 1961 by the Museum of Modern Art as "Probably the most consequential building constructed in the United States since the war," it was a principal contributor to the euhemerization of its architect.

19
Therapeutic Laboratories Addition

1964, Schlesinger & Vreeland
University Avenue, behind Hamilton Walk

20
Dining Hall and Store Complex

1969, Geddes, Brecher, Qualls & Cunningham
Spruce Street, 37th to 38th Streets

The two street fronts immediately bring to mind characteristics of two centuries of Philadelphia row houses, many of which likewise had their ground floors devoted to shops.

WP I
University of
Pennsylvania

21 Vance Hall	1971, Bower & Fradley 37th and Spruce Streets, NW corner

22
Tabernacle
Presbyterian
Church

1883-1886, Theophilus Chandler; Sunday School 1890
37th and Chestnut Streets

One of Chandler's finest ecclesiastical essays, a romantic battle of unresolved mass and overaccentuated materials is saved at the last moment by his precise detailing, resulting in an almost centrifugal unification.

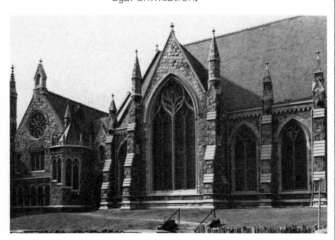

23
University
Lutheran Center

1969, Pietro Belluschi and Alexander Ewing & Associates
37th and Chestnut Streets, NE corner

24
International
House

1968, Bower & Fradley
37th and Chestnut Streets

A great arcade lying below the dormitories architecturally introduces the charming confusion of real European marketplaces.

25 Church of the Saviour	1889, rebuilt 1902, Charles M. Burns, Jr. 38th and Ludlow Streets

26 Otto Eisenlohr House	1912, Horace Trumbauer 3812 Walnut Street

These five houses (WP I 26-29), in addition to several others, have been incorporated in a new undergraduate housing block for the University (1969 by Eshbach, Pullinger, Stevens & Bruder, in association with G. Holmes Perkins and Mario Romanach).

27 Anthony Drexel House	1884, T. Roney Williamson 3809 Locust Walk Now Sigma Chi Fraternity

28 Speculative Houses for S. A. Harrison	1851, Samuel Sloan 3803, 3805 Locust Walk

29 Joseph Potts House	Ca. 1850; alterations and additions ca. 1875, The Wilson Brothers 3907 Spruce Street

30 First Church of Christ Scientist	1911, Carrère & Hastings (New York) 4012 Walnut Street

WP I

31
Philadelphia Divinity School Chapel

1925, Zantzinger, Borie & Medary
42nd and Spruce Streets

Designed in 1920 and executed by the firm over a thirty-five year period, less than half of this garden campus has seen realization. The chapel represents a fairly successful attempt to integrate Gothic and moderne verticality.

32
Spruce Hill Italianate Houses

32 A
William Barker House

1853, Samuel Sloan
4207 Walnut Street

32 B
House

Ca. 1866, John Jones, merchant builder
223 South 42nd Street

32 C
William Lofland House

1853, Samuel Sloan; alterations and additions for Adolph Borie 1911, Wilson Eyre, Jr.
4100 Pine Street

32 D
Houses

Ca. 1862, John Mitchell, merchant builder
4008-4010 Pine Street

32 E
Woodland Terrace

Ca. 1861, attributed to Samuel Sloan
Woodland Terrace, between Baltimore and Woodland Avenues

No small portion of the first wave of suburbanization of West Philadelphia consisted of these fine Italianate villas. Many were single homes of some size, but these were matched with dozens of less pretentious semidetached houses. Samuel Sloan designed a quantity of both varieties, and it is probable that he had additional influence on the others. A gratifying number still exist.

Forgiving Earth may never on these
    builders sit
Heavy as the stuff they sat on it . . . .
                                        E. Baersoudt

A large portion of West Philadelphia is
coated with a wide variety of vivacious,
and often very large, speculative row
and semidetached houses with characteristics often unique to this section of
the city. Their pretension is almost
childish, an excess remarkably self-
indulgent; they have been generally
regarded as unspeakably awful by later,
more "tasteful" generations. But it is
their very flagrance that makes them
worth some serious attention. Usually
well planned and supporting large
rooms fronted with generous verandas,
they continue to lend themselves well
to domestic needs and should be considered as key elements in future community development efforts. Groups
noted now are selected examples of a
wide variety and constitute only a
small portion of those that exist.

33 A

Rows constructed in the 1880s were
frequently reflective of the interest in
brick articulation, devoid of academic
trimmings, that was in part a result of
Furness's work. 3901-3923 Walnut
Street and 112-132 39th Street were
done for William Weightman by Willis

Hale and represent some of the more-
aggressive but least-disciplined assertions. 4200-4226 Walnut Street suggest
Furnessic idioms and possess a considerable amount of originality in
their free expression of materials.
St. Mark's Place in the middle of these
is a simpler variant and is sometimes
attributed to the firm. 4047-4061
Spruce Street and the adjoining row
on Irving Street have been attributed
to Furness (ca. 1876); awkward in proportion, they are still tightly knit in
composition. 4206-4218 Spruce Street,

probably by G. W. & W. D. Hewitt (ca. 1885), is a rare departure from the norm, wallowing blissfully in an abundance of distorted Queen Anne idioms. 318-336, 420-434 South 42nd Street are a more typical Philadelphia interpretation of the style, although apparently part of the Spruce Street development. The numerous fine twin houses that line Chester, Springfield, and Baltimore Avenues beyond Clark Park should also be noted.

33 B

Later development in the 1890s and early 1900s was slightly more inclined to academic detail but was generally no more restrained than earlier designs. The 4100 and 4200 blocks of Parkside Avenue, 3500-3520 Powelton Avenue, and 4231-4239 Walnut Street are good representatives of the most notorious products, constructed out of orange brick, frequently supporting copper trim, grossly detailed and abandoning proportion. 219-237 South 44th Street are exemplary of less ostentatious but equally awkward designs. There is little detail; the enormous bays and fractured roof line provide sufficient confusion. The 4500 and 4600 blocks of Spruce Street contain twin versions, richly detailed, which form a more cohesive block than many of the rows. 4220-4234 Spruce Street are essentially the same, this time employing mass-produced Neo-Colonial details. 4028-4036 Spruce Street are less unified.

33 C

Atypical of the area, 4108-4116 Spruce Street by Samuel Sloan, ca. 1869, is an interesting early venture in the Second Empire, more like the earlier groups in Boston's Back Bay than in Philadelphia.

WP I

34
The Woodlands,
Andrew
Hamilton House

Ca. 1742, enlarged 1788 by Andrew
Hamilton
Woodland Avenue at the end of 40th
Street
Now Offices, Woodlands Cemetery

What was a simple farmhouse was transformed by Hamilton into a magnificent
Federal country place. The early giant
portico and elaborate detailing form an
interesting contrast with the unsurfaced
fieldstone walls. While long used as
offices, the interiors are preserved and
worth noting. The barn is perhaps even
finer than the house, with its wonderfully simple use of Federal geometric
design.

 The cemetery Main Gates are by
Paul Cret (1936); the McDaniel Mau-
soleum (1874, H. Q. French) suggests
Furness somewhat awry.

35
Powelton

35 A
Henry Cochran
House

1891, Wilson Eyre, Jr.
3511 Baring Street

**35 B
Frederick G.
Thorn
House**

1883, F. G. Thorn (of The Wilson Brothers)
205 North 36th Street

This small district, bordered by Hamilton and 33rd Streets and Lancaster Avenue, forms an almost completely unspoiled early suburban neighborhood that is one of the most pleasant of its type in the city. A quantity of its Italianate villas have been attributed to Samuel Sloan. The 3600 and 3700 blocks of Hamilton Street provide good illustration of these modest endeavors while 206-208 North 35th Street is more assuming.

Many of the houses were built in the latter part of the century on an individual basis, 216 North 33rd Street being a good example. The house at 3409 Powelton Avenue, although badly altered in front, represents the only known extant Bruce Price (New York) commission in the city. While rectilinear expression was of more than passing interest to Eyre and his contemporaries, the almost cubistic simplification found in the Cochran House, similar to efforts of Chicago architects of the same period, was quite rare.

The small and unassuming scale of these residential streets is an essential buffer to the large building programs of University City. Ironically it is regarded as prime territory for progress in the form of more academic-research edifices and perhaps luxury high-rise apartments.

Roughly located along the tracks of the Pennsylvania Railroad (Mantua Avenue) between 31st and 44th Streets, Mantua contains much of the more vivacious late nineteenth-century design in the city. While it has experienced intensive decay for a number of years, the exuberance of much of the work and the sheer abundance of untouched Eastlake ornament make it well worth more than casual scrutiny.

32nd Street is probably the most interesting and varied. The ostentatious rows on the 400 block are good examples of Philadelphia High Victorian design built for Widener and Elkins in 1882 by Willis Hale. The same block of adjacent Napa Street is even more characteristic of Hale's eccentricities. Long-planned rehabilitation efforts are beginning to see fruition with quantities of magnificent detailing quickly disappearing in the process, but the finished product possesses the uninhibited proletariat vitality that has long given Baltimore its character. The 3200 block of Powelton Avenue (G. W. & W. D. Hewitt, 1882) is even more ambitious in original fabric and likewise undergoing remodeling.

The 3100 and 3200 blocks of Mount Vernon Street along with the 3200 blocks of Summer and Winter Streets are lined with smaller houses heaped with a splendid array of Stick Style bays, turrets, and porches. Part of the 400 block of North 32nd Street still retains some of the considerably earlier Italianate duplex houses. Other Romantic vestiges are found on the 800 and 900 blocks of Preston Street.

37
Presbyterian Hospital, Glover Medical Research Building

1962, Vincent Kling
39th Street and Powelton Avenue, SE corner

38
West Park Public Housing

1962, Harbeson, Hough, Livingston & Larson
44th and Market Streets

Incorporating large amounts of green space, naturally landscaped, this is one of the least sterile public housing endeavors in the city. Remains of Isaac Holden's Pennsylvania Hospital (1836-1841) were left as a reminder of what had been there.

39
The Market Street Elevated Railroad

1904-1907, Philadelphia Rapid Transit Company
Market Street, from 44th Street to Cobbs Creek; section from Schuylkill River to 44th Street demolished.

An important stimulus to the large-scale development of West Philadelphia, it is also a vital connector to the adjacent suburbs of Delaware County. The stations, which hang from the elevated tracks, are particularly intriguing. Stops are at 46th, 52nd, 56th, 60th, and 63rd Streets.

40
Paolo Busti
House

1794

Haverford Avenue at 44th Street

An attractive late Georgian house that has been sensibly integrated into the community as a recreation center.

41
Mill Creek
Public Housing

Area plan: 1946-1954, Louis Kahn, Kenneth Day, Louis E. McAllister, and Anne Tyng; Stage I (white brick) 1952, Kahn, Day, and McAllister; Stage II (red brick) 1959-1962, Louis Kahn
Fairmount Avenue, between 44th and 46th Streets

The initial project was intended as a focal point for the Mill Creek renewal area that was designed by Kahn and his associates, embodying the same neighborhood planning concepts as their work in East Poplar (see NP I 11). Like the latter, most of this never saw realization. The housing project incorporates greenways through the "informal" complex that was later adapted in Society Hill and elsewhere in the city. It is also an early attempt at integration of high-rise apartment and row houses.

43
Samuel Yellin Offices and Workshop

1915, Mellor & Meigs
5520 Arch Street
Open to the public by appointment

In the first decades of this century, Samuel Yellin produced a large quantity of ornamental metalwork of the first order. The workshop's ground floor has been preserved as a museum of his efforts.

44
Mary Elizabeth Patterson Memorial Presbyterian Church

Chapel 1885, church 1895, Theophilus Chandler
63rd and Vine Streets

42
Pennsylvania Hospital, Department for Mental and Nervous Diseases

1856-1859, Samuel Sloan; alterations and additions
49th Street, above Market Street
Now Institute of the Pennsylvania Hospital

With the enlargement in size of mental hospitals, the form of Friends Hospital (NE I 12) and Holden's earlier building (WP I 38) required adaptation to allow retention of small units in a larger institution. Dr. Thomas Kirkbride, working with Sloan, here matured the extremely influential echelon plan that stepped back small wings from the familiar center pavilion.

45
Pennsylvania
Institution
for the
Instruction
of the Blind

1897, Cope & Stewardson; additions
64th Street and Malvern Avenue

While an obvious derivative of the
University Museum (see WP I 10),
there is a shift to a more formal axis
with a suitably elaborate entrance in
addition to a more direct borrowing
of academic detail.

46
Overbrook
Farms

1893 et seq., mostly Frank and William
Price, with Boyd & Boyd, Thomas
Lonsdale, Horace Trumbauer, and
others
Overbrook Avenue and Drexel Road,
between 59th and 66th Streets; Upland
Way between Overbrook and Woodbine
Avenues; Sherwood Road between 63rd
and 66th Streets, and so on.

William Price's own house at 6334 Sherwood Drive served to attract patrons to
the new railroad suburb. 6020, 6025,
and 6054 Overbrook and 5939, 5961,
6040, and 6053 Drexel Road are some
of the most interesting structures in this
community, contemporaneous with
Pelham (see GM I 52) which many of
the same architects did for the same
developers.

47
Wynnestay,
Thomas Wynne
House

1689; 1700; additions
52nd and Woodbine Streets

One of the oldest and most distinguished of the Welsh farmers' houses that are abundant throughout the Main Line.

48
Christ Church
Hospital
(Kearsley Home)

1856-1861, John Gries
49th Street at Monument Road

A brooding early Victorian Gothic institution set off in a lovely park, it is one of a large collection of hospitals and homes in the Monument-Belmont Avenue area.

49
Philadelphia
Psychiatric
Center:
Pincus
Occupational
Therapy
Building,
Radbill
Building

1949-1953, Louis Kahn
Ford Road and Monument Avenue

**West
Philadelphia II**

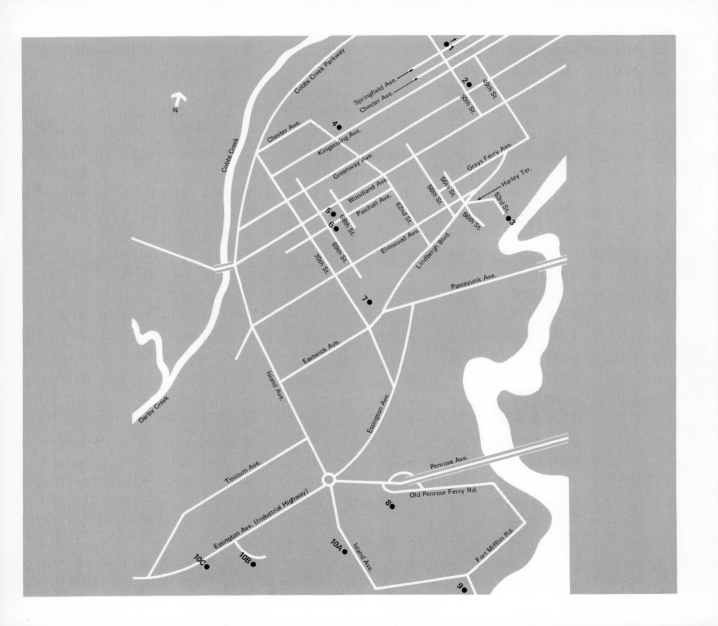

1
Church of
Saint Francis
de Sales

1906, Henry Dagit; interior alterations
1968, Venturi & Rauch; altered
4625 Springfield Avenue

2
B. B. Comegys
School

1965, Tofani & Fox
50th Street and Greenway Avenue

3
John Bartram
House

1655; 1731; 1770
Bartram Park, Lindbergh Boulevard
above 54th Street
Open to the public

A unique prerevolutionary house, its
unusual attempt at elegance on the river-
front is not dissimilar in feeling to
certain Southern California missions
with elaborate lines crudely turned.

4
Mount Moriah
Cemetery
Gatehouse

1855, Stephen Button
Cemetery Road and Kingsessing Avenue

Hoxie and Button designed a number
of cemetery buildings. Here Gothic
forms are stretched almost to the point
of caricature.

5
Saint James
Church of
Kingsessing

1762; 1854; 1875, Thomas W. Richards
6838 Woodland Avenue

6
Henry Paschall
House

Ca. 1723
6840 Paschall Avenue

7
Eastwick
Redevelopment
Area

Plan 1959, Doxiadis Associates (Athens/
Washington); buildings 1960 to present,
Doxiadis and others
Blocks adjacent to Eastwick Avenue,
above Island Avenue

Established within the tradition of the
Philadelphia row house and given a
character not unlike many grid-pattern
streets adjoining, Eastwick attempts
to add the blessings of comprehensive
planning. While it should be noted as
an effort on behalf of the city to relate
to the life-styles of the occupants,
neither the planning nor Doxiadis's
aluminum bedecked units are ultimately
successful. Open space created is generally dull, and there is a noticeable absence of either commercial or religious
focuses.

8
"Cannonball Farm"
Peter Cox House

Ca. 1668; probably completely rebuilt ca. 1715; altered
Penrose Ferry Road at Penrose Avenue Bridge (grounds of Southeast Sewage Treatment Plant)

One of the few remaining examples of early eighteenth-century farmhouses left in the city, it now sits ignominiously awaiting as yet unscheduled attention.

9
Fort Mifflin

Plan 1793, Charles L'Enfant; executed 1798, by Colonel de Toussard on the stone walls of a prerevolutionary fort; Commandant's Headquarters 1814 (or earlier); Officers' Quarters 1814; Soldiers' Barracks 1798; later buildings 1830s and 1840s
End of Fort Mifflin Road
Open to the public

After years of preservation proposals, Fort Mifflin is gradually experiencing restoration. The main and east gates recall L'Enfant's work at Fort Washington along the Potomac (1815). The Commandant's Headquarters is a fine example of Federal architecture. The fort was the site of an important, albeit little-known, battle during the Revolution which succeeded in delaying the British capture of Philadelphia.

10
Philadelphia
International
Airport

10 A
Old Municipal
Airport
Terminal

1940, Horace Castor; restaurant and
lavatories ca. 1941, Department of
Public Works, City of Philadelphia
Island Avenue, below Airport Circle

10 B
New Terminal

1953, Carroll, Grisdale & Van Alen;
additions; recent work 1968, et seq.,
Vincent Kling & Associates
Essington Avenue, below Airport Circle

10 C
TWA
Maintenance
Hangar

1954, The Ballinger Company, Ammann
& Whitney (New York), engineering
associates
Essington Avenue at Tinicum Avenue

Over the past thirty years, airports have
experienced a rapidity of change parallel
with that of the railroad station in the
latter part of the previous century. The
old complex here remains as a prime
example of terminal architecture before
the Second World War. The difference
between it and what was begun some ten
years later is quite startling. The present
building, if sterile in parts, is handsomely
proportioned and represents an early
attempt to avoid a public works image
in airport design. A new complex whose
phased erection has begun, will, in turn,
dwarf this.

Germantown

The center of Germantown grew up along one of the principal roads out of Philadelphia, Germantown Turnpike, and by 1800 the highway was lined with structures for a distance of some three miles. The great variety of buildings was generally constructed with a heterogeneous urban order contrasting the settlement with the sparsely populated farmland immediately adjacent on both sides. This pattern of growth parallels with surprising closeness mid-twentieth-century road-oriented strip communities, and for its size and early date appears to be somewhat unique. Fortunately, a large portion of the eighteenth-century town has survived, including a number of houses long regarded as some of the finer examples of this period, as well as scores of less prominent structures. Market Square is a focus for much of the restoration, which has adhered to an agreeable policy of preservation for use. Today Germantown remains as a commercial core incorporating development of almost three hundred years, living with, rather than in, the past.

The mid-nineteenth century saw the surrounding farmland gradually transformed into suburbs for many leading Philadelphians as well as Germantown families. While most of the largest Romantic and High Victorian villas have been demolished with later developments, Walnut Lane and Tulpehocken Street above Wayne Avenue as well as East Penn Street provide a good idea of what a sizable portion of Germantown was once like. With the development of commuter railroad lines through Germantown to Chestnut Hill by the Pennsylvania and Reading, housing began to fill in the remaining open space through new communities such as Pelham. Pleasant late nineteenth- and early twentieth-century suburban enclaves of this nature now comprise a large part of the area.

Much of the important work in the area since the turn of the century occurred in the vicinity of Chestnut Hill. Development began in the 1880s under the direction of Henry Howard Houston, who erected a hotel and church as well as a number of substantial houses. But the more significant improvements were made in the first part of this century by his son-in-law, Dr. George Woodward, with the developments around Lincoln Drive, Winston Street, and the French Village. Architecturally they were executed with unusual sophistication, designed as unobtrusive enhancements to the picturesque townscape, but as works of suburban planning they were perhaps even more valuable contributions as prototypes for residential design elsewhere in the United States in the years that followed. Other contemporaneous building also frequently took advantage of the limited size and often irregular topography of the sites in attempting to achieve a fusion of urban and rural character. A large body of work by the principal residential architects in the city has left the area with one of the more important assemblages of early twentieth-century traditional domestic architecture in this country. If recent work has been limited, some of it has been of equal caliber.

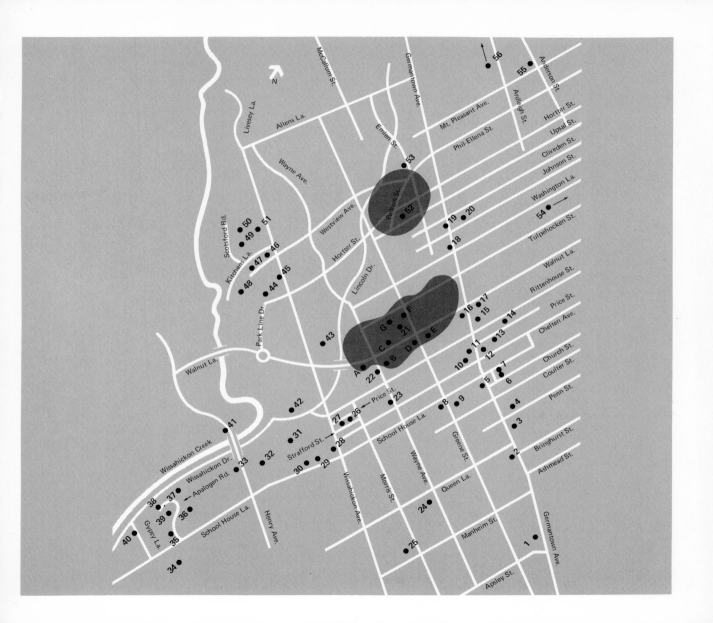

1
Loudoun,
Thomas Armat
House

Ca. 1801; portico added later
4650 Germantown Avenue

In addition to those noted separately, the number of eighteenth- and early nineteenth-century structures along Germantown Avenue is quite impressive. Many of the more interesting of these buildings are listed here:

4821 Menhl House, ca. 1800
4825 Ottinger House, ca. 1785
5269 Grumblethorpe Tenant House, ca. 1741
5275 Clarkson-Watson House, ca. 1778
5300 Trinity Church House, 1760
5430 John Ashmead House, ca. 1796?
5434 William Ashmead House, ca. 1740
5448 Bringhurst House
5450 Thomas Armat House, ca. 1792
5938 Engle House, 1759
6112 Dirick Jansen House
6119 Mennonite Meeting House, 1770
6313 Concord Schoolhouse, 1775
6358 Sproengell House, ca. 1773?
6500 Bardsley House, ca. 1770
6504 Daniel Bilmire House, ca. 1790
6505-6507 Michael Bilmire House, ca. 1730
6514 Christopher Mason House, 1765, front 1798; 1880
6669 Beggarstown School, ca. 1740
7402 Garrett Rittenhouse House, ca. 1804
7413 John Hyatt House, ante 1739

2
Germantown
Historical
Society

2 A
Baynton House

1802
5208 Germantown Avenue

2 B
Conyngham-
Hacker
House

1745 et seq.
5214 Germantown Avenue

2 C
Howell House

Ca. 1795
5218 Germantown Avenue

Three nicely related houses that now
contain many of the archives as well as
furnishings of the eighteenth- and early
nineteenth-century community

3
Grumblethorpe,
John Wistar
House

1744; additions 1794; alterations 1808;
restored to 1744 appearance
5261 Germantown Avenue

Restored within the last few years, this
is probably the most illustrious example
of early eighteenth-century design in
Germantown.

GM I

4
East Penn Street

4 A **Ivy Lodge**	Ca. 1850, style of Samuel Sloan 29 East Penn Street
4 B **Charles Willing House**	Ca. 1885, style of T. Roney Williamson 51 East Penn Street

A number of surprisingly large houses remain on the pleasant block directly east of Germantown Avenue.

5
Deschler-Perot-Morris House

1772
5442 Germantown Avenue
Open to the public

6
Fromberger House

1795
5501 Germantown Avenue
Now Germantown Fire Insurance Company

Skillfully restored and adapted for use as offices, it has been a model for other similar projects along the old Pike.

7
West Market Square Presbyterian Church

1839; 1857; additions and alterations 1882, 1884, 1888, style of T. Roney Williamson
5515 Germantown Avenue

An effective interpretation of Romanesque and Queen Anne Revivals, with stylistic elements that are frequently characteristic of Williamson's work

8
Union
School House
(Germantown
Academy)

1760
School House Lane and Greene Street
Now Lutheran Academy

When Benjamin Franklin and other well-meaning Philadelphians proposed a school in Germantown for the "ignorant Deutsch," the residents decided to start one of their own.

9
Second Church
of Christ
Scientist

1918-1925, Day & Klauder
5443 Greene Street

10
Vernon,
James Matthews
House

Before 1741; enlarged 1805
Vernon Park, Germantown Avenue
above Chelten Avenue

One of the few early houses that was set back from the Pike. its immediate property now forms a pleasant park (Bissell & Sinkler, 1914).

GM I

11
**Free Library
of Philadelphia,
Germantown/
Vernon Park
Branch**

1895, Frank Miles Day & Brother
Vernon Park

Architects in the early stages of the
Colonial Revival were often more concerned with their own interpretations
of Georgian details than they were in
understanding the discipline of the style.
While this building is hardly of the proportions known to the eighteenth-
century builders, it does express a then
rare sympathy with their work.

12
**Germantown and
Chestnut Hill
Railroad
Station**

1855
5735 Germantown Avenue
Now stores

13
**First Baptist
Church**

1852, Samuel Sloan
40 East Price Street
Now Polite Temple Baptist Church

14
**Saint Vincent's
Parish Hall**

1884, possibly Hazelhurst & Huckel
Price Street, above Lena Street

Though the building contains Furnessic
features, the front is awkward and ama-
teurishly handled; the weather vane
is a prize. Hazelhurst had trained in the
Furness office.

15
Green Tree
Tavern

1748
6019 Germantown Avenue
Now First Methodist Church office and parish hall

16
Wyck,
Hans Millan
House

Ca. 1690; ca. 1720; center section and alterations 1824, William Strickland for Ruben Haines
6026 Germantown Avenue

Strickland combined two small dwellings bridging an old Indian path, noticeably in keeping with traditional design, suggesting both his appreciation of the Georgian and the strength of that style's influence.

GM I

17
The Laurens,
Shippen-Blair
House

Before 1775; doorway from the Bensell
House (ca. 1795) installed 1880
6043 Germantown Avenue

18
John Johnson
House

1765
6306 Germantown Avenue

19
Upsala,
Dirick Jansen
House

Ca. 1755; additions 1798-1801 for
John Johnson
6430 Germantown Avenue
Open to the public

What is probably Germantown's prime
example of Federal architecture is,
nonetheless, well rooted in Georgian
precedent.

20
Cliveden,
Benjamin Chew
House

1761-1767, Jacob Knorr and Benjamin
Chew
6401 Germantown Avenue
Open to the public

One of the great Philadelphia country
houses, Cliveden remained in the Chew
family until 1972, and has seen few significant alterations. The noteworthy
front hall, with an unusually early use
of Tuscan columns, hosted a portion of
the Battle of Germantown (1777).

21
**Walnut Lane/
Tulpehocken
Street**

These streets between Germantown and Wayne Avenues are a microcosm of many of the Philadelphia approaches to suburban domestic design from the mid-nineteenth century to the early twentieth and form what is one of the most significant groupings of local architecture. While numerous deserving structures throughout Germantown have not been included, most types extant are well represented here. Remarkably, these streets have not suffered significant change, and efforts should be continued to ensure their maintenance as a unit.

**21 A
Edmund
Crenshaw
House**

1891, 1900, Cope & Stewardson
420 West Walnut Lane

**21 B
Henry Listar
Townsend
House**

1887
6015 Wayne Avenue

**21 C
William
Shelmerdine
House**

1899, Rankin & Kellogg
269 West Walnut Lane

21 D
House

Ca. 1856, attributed to Samuel Sloan
200 West Walnut Lane

21 E
House

Ca. 1860, attributed to Samuel Sloan;
stable altered by Walter Mellor (of
Mellor & Meigs) for himself 1912 and
1916
150 West Walnut Lane

The Crenshaw House shows the evolving of a personal style by Cope & Stewardson which, while bearing some resemblance to Eyre's, is neither as developed nor as cohesive. The rectilinear characteristics of Hazlehurst & Huckel's John Reator House at 210 Walnut Lane are derived from Eyre's town houses. The Townsend House has the undisciplined Teutonic rusticity common and somewhat peculiar to Philadelphia suburban dwellings of the High Victorian era. Similarly ponderous in their proportions and selection of adornment are 274, 270, and 264 Walnut Lane around the corner. 258 and 266 Tulpehocken, designed by Addison Hutton in 1880, are slightly more conservative variations of the same mood. 200 and 150 Walnut Lane are two of the finest houses of the early Romantic period in greater Philadelphia. Such achievements as the scalings of these small houses so that they might appear as considerably larger rural villas further suggest that a man of Sloan's ability was involved. 251, 155,

21 F
Ebenezer
Maxwell
House

1859, attributed to Joseph Hoxie
200 West Tulpehocken Street

21 G
Henry
Cummings
House

1892, Frank Miles Day & Brother
240 West Tulpehocken Street

146, 143, 138, and 131 Walnut Lane and 9, 26, 29, 30-32, 43-45, 53, 59, 120, 128, 136, 141, 154, and 223-225 Tulpehocken are various forms of more modest Gothic Revival and Italianate design, many with a wealth of gingerbread ornament. A number of others support later alterations in High Victorian fancies. The Cummings House is an interesting contemporary of Cope & Stewardson's early work. 239 Walnut Lane, while outwardly similar, has little of Day's delicate asymmetrical balance or finesse of detail. 246 Tulpehocken is a stodgy late Queen Anne Revival house probably also of ca. 1890. 201 Tulpehocken is an early Georgian Revival, still owing some allegiance to the Shingle Style. Germantown architects Mantle Fielding and George Pearson did numerous buildings of this variety. 28 Walnut Lane was converted from a barn of Wyck by Fielding for his own use about 1910. 115 Tulpehocken is perhaps a more common type for Philadelphia with simple, tightly knit elements taken from the more anonymous prototypes of the style. H. Louis Duhring designed many houses in Germantown of like character. 50 Walnut Lane and 235 Tulpehocken are further variations of the Georgian. The Shelmerdine House is of a considerably more formal Georgian style often used by Horace Trumbauer.

GM I

22
Saint Peter's
Church

1873, George Hewitt (of Furness & Hewitt); chancel 1896, parish house 1898, G. W. and W. D. Hewitt
Wayne Avenue and Harvey Streets

23
Clarence
Pickett
Middle School

1968, Geddes, Brecher, Qualls & Cunningham
Wayne Avenue, from Chelten to Rittenhouse Streets

A vast brutal series of slabs detailed as if some modern-day fortress, it painfully reflects the nature of many urban schools.

24
Sally Watson
House

1889, Wilson Eyre, Jr.
5128 Wayne Avenue

25
Germantown
Cricket Club

1890, wings 1902, bowling alley 1907
McKim, Mead & White (New York)
Manheim and Morris Streets

White's early but mature rendering of the Georgian Revival inevitably had an influence on the nature of subsequent work in the area.

26
Harriet
Schaeffer
House

1888, Wilson Eyre, Jr.; additions ca.
1920 Wilson, Harris & Richards
433 Stafford Street

Stretched lengthwise across one end of
the narrow site to obtain maximum
open space, this residence has a free
and open plan characteristic of the best
Shingle Style work. It is indicative of
the architect's ability to work deftly
with demanding restrictions and should
be considered one of his best early
works.

27
House

Alterations and additions to what was
probably a stable, 1894, 1904, Wilson
Eyre, Jr.
441 Stafford Street

28
Alden Park
Apartments

1920, et seq., Edwyn Rorke
Wissahickon Avenue and School House
Lane

An early example of freestanding apartment towers, the semipicturesque architecture is of less importance than the
success achieved in adapting high-den-
sity dwelling units to a park setting.
The J. C. Strawbridge House (1885,
Addison Hutton) was altered and
incorporated into the development
as a restaurant.

29
Edward Steel
House

Extensive additions and alterations to an earlier dwelling 1875, library and conservatory 1883, Addison Hutton; interior alterations ca. 1890, Mantle Fielding
3001 School House Lane

30
Lycoming,
William Turner
House

1907, Wilson Eyre, Jr.; alterations and additions
3005 School House Lane
Now Lycoming House

As if a farmhouse set picturesquely along one corner of the property, it was a prototype of Eyre's most sublime early twentieth-century work as well as the inclinations of the following generation. Much of the subtlety of its detail and relationship to the land has been marred, but the geometry of its chimney and flock of gables as viewed from the garage court remains artlessly serene.

31
Kenneth
Hasserick
House

1957, Richard Neutra (Los Angeles) and Thaddeus Longstreth (Princeton); later additions
3033 School House Lane

32
Library
Building,
Philadelphia
College
of Textiles
and Science

1966, Alexander Ewing & Associates
School House Lane and Henry Avenue

33
Isaac Levy
House

1935, George Howe
4150 Henry Avenue
Now Germantown Laboratories, Franklin Institute

A curious return to a semitraditional approach—with moderne touches, it reflects Howe's ponderous struggle to relate the two seemingly disparate schools.

34
William
Weightman
House

1887, style of Willis Hale or Mantle
Fielding
3480 School House Lane
Now Ravenhill Academy

35
Tulipwood,
Horace Fleisher
House

1954, Roth & Fleisher
4030 Apalogen Road

While good modern architecture in Philadelphia during the late 1940s and 1950s was generally a rare occurrence, Apalogen Road and adjacent Gypsy Lane provide a substantial number of exceptions and contain a wide variety of approaches to good domestic design of that era.

36
Charles Oller
House

1955, Frank Weise
4101 Apalogen Road

37
N. William
Winkelman, Jr.,
House

1958, Montgomery & Bishop
4141 Apalogen Road

38
George Starrels
House

1958, James Reid Thomson
4165 Apalogen Road

GM I

39
Robert Brasler House

1966, Joel Levinson
4122 Apalogen Road

40
Wissahickon Hall

1849
Wissahickon Drive and Gypsy Lane
Now Fairmount Park Guardhouse

41
Henry Avenue Bridge

1927, Paul Cret; Modjeski, Master & Chase, engineers
Henry Avenue over the Wissahickon Valley

A powerful design that lends a moment of sublime drama when approached from the Wissahickon Drive.

42
Rittenhouse Cottage

1707, for William Rittenhouse
Lincoln Drive at the foot of Rittenhouse Street

Rittenhouse built the first paper mill in the country in 1690 on the adjacent property. Surviving associated buildings (built later) may help give an impression of early industrial enclaves.

43
George Thomas
House

1864
6245 Wissahickon Avenue
Now in Fairmount Park

A heavy Gothic villa, somewhat Germanic in feeling, it is the last large Romantic country house left in Germantown. While elements in the building suggest it might have been designed by Sloan, it is more likely derived from his well-publicized work.

44
Abraham
Malmed
House

1928, Mellor, Meigs & Howe
1021 Hortter Street

A parting work with Mellor and Meigs, it shows Howe's interest in flat surfaces, accentuating their planar qualities. His influence in the firm can be seen by comparison with the Leeds House (GM I 47) designed the next year.

45
Spring Bank,
Matthias Jacobs
House

Ca. 1730; numerous additions and alterations
Wissahickon Avenue above Hortter Street

Spring Bank forms a good example of the growth patterns of many old Philadelphia country houses. While a large portion of these have been restored or at least redesigned to resemble better their early days, this still has the charm of years of accumulation. Some of the later additions have distinct Furnessic character and may have been by him.

GM I

46
Garth,
Robert
McCracken
House

1919, 1926, Mellor, Meigs & Howe
1009 Westview Avenue

Situated on a very restricted site, house and garden have been beautifully integrated. The architects were as accomplished working with a small, intimate structure such as this as they were with large country places.

47
Morris Leeds
House

1929-1935; Mellor & Meigs
1025 Westview Avenue

48
The Monastery,
Joseph Gorgas
House

Ca. 1746; porch added later
End of Kitchens Lane (Fairmount Park)

The unusual form of rural design has led to the house's name, although it was probably never an actual monastery.

49
Garth Gwyn,
Walter Mellor
House

Ca. 1928, Mellor, Meigs & Howe
Scotsford Road

50
Herbert Morris
House

1927, Edmund Gilchrist
End of Scotsford Road

Gilchrist's domestic work through
the 1920s grew increasingly formal,
although he always looked to rural
architecture for precedent. The difference, even in the siting, from works
of Mellor, Meigs & Howe such as the
McCracken House (see GM I 46),
should be noted.

51
Adelbert Fisher
House

1909, Milton Medary
6904 Wissahickon Avenue

Examples of designs so clearly in the
Art Nouveau are rare in this country,
and it does not seem to have been a
continuing or serious interest for
Medary.

GM I

52
Pelham

One of several communities developed around the stations of the Pennsylvania Railroad extension, it is representative of some of the better suburban planning of the late nineteenth century (compare with Overbrook Farms, WP I 46). Some of the more interesting houses, most of them designed by Keen & Mead, include
235 Pelham Street
330 Pelham Street
6700 Cresheim Street
6701 Cresheim Street
305 Upsal Street
131-133 Phil-Ellena Street
34-36 Phil-Ellena Street
255 Hortter Street
305 Hortter Street
336-338 Hortter Street

The influence of Wilson Eyre can be seen in addition to some rather dubious innuendos concerning the Georgian and other period revivals.

The station on Greene Street at the foot of Upsal, built about 1884 and probably designed by The Wilson Brothers, is a variation of many on the same branch of the railroad.

53
James Hackett
House

1887, Cope & Stewardson
6720 Emlen Street
Now Mt. Airy Children's House

54
Houses for
Francis Cope

54 A   1886, Cope & Stewardson
Double House 6012-6014 Chew Street

54 B   Ca. 1887, Cope & Stewardson
House   first dwelling on the private road
                  adjacent to Awbury

Amid what was the Cope family's
homestead (now partially opened as
the Awbury Arboretum) these are
two especially handsome Shingle
Style works among several in the neighborhood designed by the firm.

55   1883, probably Furness & Evans
Sedgwick   Mt. Pleasant Avenue and Reading
Station   Railroad

56   1883, probably Furness & Evans
Mount Airy   Gowen Street and Reading Railroad
Station
                 These stations, although almost surely
                 by Furness's hand, have still not been
                 documented (compare with Wissahickon
                 Station, NP III 6).

Germantown II

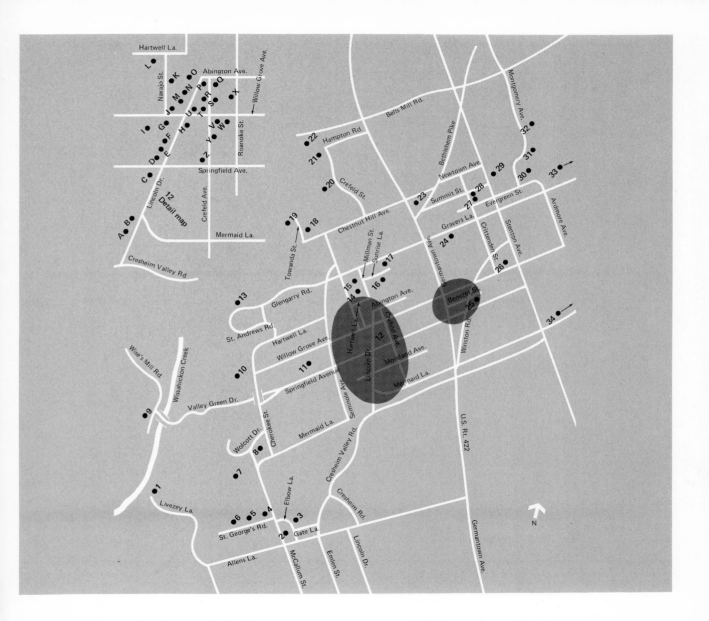

GM II

1
Glenfern,
Thomas
Shoemaker
House
(The Livesey
House)

Ca. 1690-ca. 1725
Livezey Lane and Wissahickon Creek
(Fairmount Park)
Now Valley Green Canoe Club

2
Thomas Todd
House

1966, Wallace, McHarg, Roberts &
Todd
7321 McCallum Street

3
French Village

1925-1928, Robert McGoodwin (7321
Elbow Lane, by Willing, Sims & Talbut)
Elbow and Gate Lanes, off Allens Lane

A small development of houses for the
Woodward estate which converts an
awkward piece of land into a cohesive,
yet intimate, series of picturesque enclaves. The houses are set on small
private roads open to adjacent Fairmount Park, rather than bordering on
thoroughfares.

4
Cogshill,
Jessie W. Smith
House

1915, Edmund Gilchrist
601 St. Georges Road

5
Cogslea,
Violet Oakley
House and
Studio

Remodeling of early farmhouse 1902,
Frank Miles Day & Brother; Studio
added to ca. 1920.
615 St. Georges Road
Studio: 627 St. Georges Road (now
Lower Cogslea, the Violet Oakley Memorial Foundation)

The regional group was one of the first
serious attempts at returning to the
eighteenth-century Pennsylvania farmhouse for idioms. The lofty studios
of the noted painter have been kept
beautifully intact, recalling another era
of the avant-garde.

6
Charles Day
House

Ca. 1927, Willing, Sims & Talbut
631 St. Georges Road

GM II

7
Krisheim,
George
Woodward
House

1910, Peabody & Stearns (Boston);
gardener's cottage 1908, Wilson Eyre,
Jr.
McCallum Street at the end of Mermaid
Lane
Now Study Center of the Board of
Christian Education, United Presby-
terian Church

8
Cherokee
Village

1955, 1959, Oskar Stonorov
End of McCallum Street

While not executed in keeping with
the character of earlier developments,
this makes maximum use of the land
under its own standards, which, if
more formal, are equally practical.

9
Inn at
Valley Green

Ca. 1850
End of Valley Green Road (Fairmount
Park)

Once a host to travelers, it is still open
for meals and is located in one of the
loveliest sections of the park.

10
Druim Moir,
Henry Howard
Houston
House

1886, G. W. & W. D. Hewitt; gardens
1921, Robert McGoodwin; altered
End of Willow Grove Avenue
Now Houston Foundation

A complete rebuilding of an earlier
Notman work, Mr. Houston's house
was considered the finest in Philadelphia
for some years. The removal of the
towers in 1952 now gives the exterior
a curiously modern feeling.

11
Wissahickon
Inn

1884, G. W. & W. D. Hewitt
Willow Grove Avenue and Huron Street
Now Chestnut Hill Academy

An "English Inn" was part of Houston's
initial development of Chestnut Hill. He
was also responsible for the erection of
the nearby Church of Saint Martin-in-
the-Fields in 1888 by the same architects (addition 1900, Theophilus
Chandler).

12
Lincoln Drive
Development

An early attempt at planned suburban development, surely influenced by the Garden City Movement, the Lincoln Drive Development should be noted as one of the most successful projects of its nature in the country. The astute relationships established between the various units and their sites, along with the noticeable lack of preciousness (which so often plagued residential work in the early 1900s), reflect the architects' profound sensibilities to the intricacies of both planning and building design. The naturalness achieved within a complex structure is in much the same spirit as the eighteenth-century English garden. Three architectural firms were involved in effecting the whole in stages over a period of some twenty years.

While the project appears to have been extremely influential on ensuing work in the nation, others seldom achieved the same results.

12 A **Robert** **McGoodwin** **House**	1916, Robert McGoodwin 7620 Lincoln Drive
12 B **Ross House**	1916, Robert McGoodwin 7700 Lincoln Drive
12 C **Twin Houses**	1906, Duhring, Okie & Ziegler 7800-7818 Lincoln Drive
12 D **Willet** **Stained Glass** **Company** **Studio**	1914-1925, Duhring, Okie & Ziegler 7900-7906 Lincoln Drive
12 E **Edward Clark III** **House**	1917, Duhring, Okie & Ziegler 7922 Lincoln Drive
12 F **Rodman House**	1917, Robert McGoodwin 7924 Lincoln Drive
12 G **Sulgrave Manor**	1927, H. Louis Duhring 200 West Willow Grove Avenue
12 H **Half Moon** **Houses**	1917, Duhring, Okie & Ziegler 7919-7925 Lincoln Drive

| 12 I | 1916, Robert McGoodwin |
| House | 224 Willow Grove Avenue |

| 12 J | 1915, Robert McGoodwin |
| Houses | 131-135 West Willow Grove Avenue |

| 12 K | 1917, Edmund Gilchrist |
| Houses | 8005-8019 Navajo Street |

| 12 L | 1928, Robert McGoodwin |
| House | 300 West Hartwell Lane |

12 M	1920, Robert McGoodwin
Norman Ellison	8004 Lincoln Drive
House	

| 12 N | 1917, Robert McGoodwin |
| House | 8008 Lincoln Drive |

12 O	1928, Robert McGoodwin
W. Frazier III	8010 Lincoln Drive
House	

| 12 P | 1916, Robert McGoodwin |
| House | 8014 Crefeld Avenue |

| 12 Q | 1914, Edmund Gilchrist |
| Double House | 116-118 West Abington Avenue |

| 12 R | 1921, Edmund Gilchrist |
| Three Houses | 8008-8012 Crefeld Avenue |

| 12 S | 1913, Edmund Gilchrist |
| Houses | 8001-8013 Crefeld Avenue |

GM II

12 T House	1916, Edmund Gilchrist 8000 Crefeld Avenue
12 U Linden Court	1916, Edmund Gilchrist 103-113 West Willow Grove Avenue

13 Mrs. Thomas Raeburn White House	1963, Mitchell/Giurgola Associates 717 West Glengarry Road

12 V Double House	1910, McGoodwin & Hawley 56-58 West Willow Grove Avenue
12 W Houses	1915, Duhring, Okie & Ziegler 42-52 West Willow Grove Avenue
12 X Roanoke Court	1931, H. Louis Duhring 8014-8028 Roanoke Street
12 Y Double House	1911 7913-7915 Crefeld Avenue
12 Z House	1912, Edmund Gilchrist 101 West Springfield Avenue

14
Charles
Woodward
House

1939, Kenneth Day; later additions
8220 Millman Street

As with George Howe, Day was trained
in the Beaux Arts and similarly shifted
his efforts in the 1930s with an attempt
at integration of the International Style
principals with regional design. The
interior here is a particularly happy
unification of flowing, yet reasonably
formal, spaces.

15
Mrs. Robert
Venturi, Sr.,
House

1962, Venturi & Short
8330 Millman Street

16
Margaret
Esherick
House

1960, Louis Kahn
204 Sunrise Lane

17
Guenther
Buchholz
House

1967, Guenther Buchholz
201 Sunrise Lane

The strong sculpturesque volumes and
rich exploitation of wood recall the
California work of Harwell Harris and
Rudolph Schindler.

GM II

18
J. Wilmer Biddle
House

Ca. 1905, Cope & Stewardson
455 Chestnut Hill Avenue

Both Cope & Stewardson and Frank
Miles Day designed a number of houses
that, like those of their English contemporaries, were as much an abstract
rectilinear statement as an exhibition
of Jacobean details.

19
Norton Downs
House

1925, Robert McGoodwin
8840 Towanda Avenue

20
Schofield
Andrews
House

1930, Tilden, Register & Pepper
9002 Crefeld Avenue

21
Mrs. B. Franklin
Pepper House

1920, Willing and Sims
9120 Crefeld Avenue

22
High Hollow,
George Howe
House

1914, George Howe (of Furness, Evans & Company); alterations and pool 1928 for Samuel Crozer, George Howe; further interior alterations 1929, Howe & Lescaze
101 West Hampton Road

Howe's first major work, the house follows Eyre's precedent in evolving an anonymity from local as well as European sources of a similar nature. If some of the fusions are awkward, it is nonetheless a sensitive building, and it became one of the prototypes of Pastoral design.

23
Saint Paul's
Church

Chapel (now auditorium) 1882, James Sims; parish house 1888, Cope & Stewardson; new church and school 1928, Zantzinger, Borie & Medary
22 East Chestnut Hill Avenue

Picturesque ecclesiastical buildings are joined enthusiastically by a late "high church" monument.

GM II

24
Gravers Station

1883, Furness & Evans
Gravers Lane and Reading Railroad

Of the numerous suburban stations by
or attributed to Furness, this is one
of the finest, extravagantly displaying
his love of abstracted and stylized High
Victorian forms, and the only one with
actual documentation as to his involve-
ment.

25
Winston Road
Development

25 A
Winston Court

1925, H. Louis Duhring
7821-7909 Winston Road

25 B
Houses

1920, Robert McGoodwin
7830-7832 Winston Road, 22-32 East
Springfield Avenue

25 C
Benezet Street
Houses

1910-1916, Duhring, Okie & Ziegler
Benezet Street and Springfield Avenue,
Germantown Avenue to Winston Road

A considerably more modest endeavor
than either the French Village or the
development along Lincoln Drive, it
reveals Woodward's diversity of interests
in producing good housing. Duhring's
four-unit houses, two on each street,
provide an agreeable and inexpensive
alternative to the monotony of row
houses, providing low density while still
maintaining the economy of space
characteristic of housing in the city. A
similar group done by Woodward with
Duhring as architect is located on
Carleton and Nippon Streets in Mount
Airy. These experimental but successful
works seem to have had some impact
upon speculative projects in other parts
of the city, but developers had more
interest in Duhring's picturesque facades
than the sensibility of his planning.

26
Joseph
Burroughs
House

1888, Wilson Eyre, Jr.; altered
399 Willow Grove Avenue

27
Anglecot,
Charles Potter
House

1883, 1886, 1887, 1889, 1896, 1901,
1910, Wilson Eyre, Jr.; alterations and
additions

Evergreen Street and Prospect Avenue
Now Anglecot Sanitorium

Originally a handsome early Shingle
Style house, its multitude of enlarge-
ments and alterations reflect Eyre's
shifting attitudes toward design. If not
entirely cohesive, it is still a notable
study in asymmetry. The interiors (of
various dates) are mostly intact and
well worth scrutiny.

28
C. Watson
House

Ca. 1854; additions and alterations for
Spencer Janney after 1870
100 Summit Street

What initially may have been an Italianate villa is coated with an assemblage
of early High Victorian paraphernalia.

29
Brookfield,
Jay Cooke III
House

1909, 1914, Wilson Eyre, Jr.; alterations
Stenton Avenue and Newton Road, NW
corner, Montgomery County
Now Institutes for the Achievement of
Human Potential

30
Persifor
Frazer III
House

1921, Robert McGoodwin
Montgomery Avenue and Evergreen
Street, Montgomery County

31
Walter West, Jr.,
House

1949, Bishop & Wright
8725 Montgomery Avenue, Montgomery
County

32
Ropsley,
Francis
McIlhenny
House

1918, et seq., Mellor, Meigs & Howe
Montgomery Avenue, Montgomery
County

A close integration of a cultivated landscape, including outbuildings, with the
main house was one of the architects'
accomplished achievements.

33
Mrs. Samuel
Rotan
House

1927, Robert McGoodwin, gardener's cottage and garage, Wilson Eyre & McIlvaine
End of Flourtown Road, Montgomery County
Now University of Pennsylvania Conference Center

Although archaeological reconstructions of European prototypes were popular elsewhere in the country in the 1920s, there were few built in the Philadelphia area. This interesting exception was especially unusual for the architects involved, although the informal aspects of the plan seem to have become a primary emphasis.

34
Robert
Montgomery
Brown
House

1934, Robert Montgomery Brown
Linden Road, Montgomery County

Demolished Buildings

During the five years of active preparation of this book the following buildings have been deleted from the manuscript because of demolition or extensively disfiguring alterations.

Center City

Jackson Building, ca. 1845, John Notman, 418 Arch Street. Demolished 1969.

George Drexel Childs House, 1869, John McArthur, Jr., 22nd and Walnut Streets. Demolished 1970.

Schuylkill Navy Athletic Club, 1889, Moses & King, designers, Willis Hale, facade, 1626 Arch Street. Demolished 1971.

Bank of North America, 1893, James H. Windrim, 311 Chestnut Street. Demolished 1972.

Alexander Cassatt House, alterations to an 1856 structure ca. 1890, probably by The Wilson Brothers, 202 West Rittenhouse Square. Demolished 1972.

J. B. Lippincott House, 1869, Addison Hutton, 204 West Rittenhouse Square. Demolished 1972.

Fairmount Park

Girard Avenue Bridge, 1872, T. Clark, engineer, Henry and James Sims, architects, Schuylkill River at Girard Avenue. Demolished 1970.

North Philadelphia

Philadelphia and Reading Railroad, North Broad Street Station, ca. 1920, Horace Trumbauer, Broad Street at Huntingdon Street. Badly altered 1970.

Home for Aged and Infirm Israelites, 1888, Furness, Evans & Company, Einstein Medical Center, Broad Street and Tabor Road. Demolished 1971.

A. F. L. Medical Service Plan Clinic, 1954, Louis Kahn, 1326 Vine Street. Demolished 1973.

The Northeast

Benjamin Rush Birthplace, ca. 1690-ca. 1850, Rayland Road and East Keswick Street. Demolished by mistake 1969. Much debris recovered from landfill. Reconstruction proposed elsewhere.

South Philadelphia

Philadelphia County (Moyamensing) Prison, 1832 and 1836, Thomas U. Walter, Reed and 10th Streets. Demolished 1968.

Prince of Peace Church, 1901, 1906, Furness, Evans & Company, 22nd and Morris Streets. Demolished 1972.

West Philadelphia

Lea House, ca. 1850, 3903 Spruce Street. Demolished 1969.

John Harrison Chemistry Laboratories, University of Pennsylvania, 1893, Cope & Stewardson, 34th and Spruce Streets. Demolished 1970.

Germantown

Compton, John Morris House, 1887, Theophilus Chandler, Morris Arboretum, Chestnut Hill. Demolished 1968.

Selected Bibliography and Sources

Books and Monographs

American Institute of Architects, Philadelphia Chapter
Philadelphia Architecture. New York: Reinhold, 1961.

American Philosophical Society
Historic Philadelphia from the Founding until the Early Nineteenth Century. Philadelphia: American Philosophical Society, 1953.

Archambault, Anne Margarette
A Guide Book of Art, Architecture and Historic Interests in Pennsylvania. Philadelphia: Winston, 1924.

Brandt, Francis Burke
The Wissahickon Valley within the City of Philadelphia. Philadelphia: Corn Exchange National Bank, 1927.

Brandt, Francis Burke, and Gummere, Henry Volkmar
Byways and Boulevards in and about Historic Philadelphia. Philadelphia: Corn Exchange National Bank, 1925

Dallett, Francis James
An Architectural View of Washington Square. Philadelphia: n.p., 1968.

Delaware Valley Regional Planning Commission
Inventory of Historic Sites. Philadelphia: Delaware Valley Regional Planning Commission, 1970.

Detweiler, Willard S., Jr
Chestnut Hill, and Architectural History. Philadelphia: Chestnut Hill Historical Society, 1969.

Dickson, H.
A Hundred Pennsylvania Buildings. State College, Pennsylvania: Pennsylvania State University Press, 1954.

Eberlein, Harold Donaldson, and Hubbard, Cortlandt Van Dyke
Portrait of a Colonial City: Philadelphia 1670-1838. Philadelphia: Lippincott, 1939.

Eberlein, Harold Donaldson, and Lippincott, Horace Mather
The Colonial Homes of Philadelphia and Its Neighborhood. Philadelphia: Lippincott, 1912.

Edgell, George H.
The American Architecture of Today. New York: Scribners, 1928.

Faris, John T.
Old Roads out of Philadelphia. Philadelphia: Lippincott, 1917.

Faris, John T.
Old Churches and Meeting Houses in and around Philadelphia. Philadelphia: Lippincott, 1926.

Gallagher, H. M. Pierce
Robert Mills. New York: Columbia
University Press, 1935.

Gilchrist, Agnes Addison
William Strickland: Architect and
Engineer, 1788-1854. Philadelphia:
University of Pennsylvania Press, 1950;
additional text published as a supple-
ment to the Journal of the Society of
Architectural Historians, October 1954.

Hamlin, Talbot F.
Benjamin Henry Latrobe. New York:
Oxford University Press, 1955.

Hotchkin, Rev. S. F.
Ancient and Modern Germantown, Mt.
Airy and Chestnut Hill. Philadelphia:
P. W. Ziegler & Co., 1889.

Hotchkin, Rev. S. F.
The York Road, Old and New; Fox
Chase and Vicinity; Bustleton and
Vicinity. Philadelphia: Binder & Kelly,
1892.

Hotchkin, Rev. S. F.
The Bristol Pike. Philadelphia:
George W. Jacobs & Co., 1893.

Jackson, Joseph
Early Philadelphia Architects and
Engineers. Philadelphia: J. Jackson, 1923.

Jackson, Joseph
America's Most Historic Highway:
Market Street, Philadelphia.
Philadelphia: Wanamaker, 1926.

King, Moses
Philadelphia and Notable Philadelphians.
New York: Moses King, 1901.

Levy, Alan G.; Wurman, Richard S.;
and Chapman, William B.
Our Man-Made Environment: Book 7.
Philadelphia: Group for Environmental
Education, 1969.

Lippincott, Horace Mather
Quaker Meetinghouses and a Little
Humor. Jenkintown: Old York Road
Publishing Co., 1952.

McCall, Elizabeth B.
Old Philadelphia Houses on Society Hill.
New York: Architectural Book Publish-
ing Co., 1966.

McGoodwin, Robert R.
Monograph of the Work of Robert R.
McGoodwin. Philadelphia: William Fell
Co., 1942.

Massey, James C., ed.
Two Centuries of Philadelphia Architectural Drawings. Philadelphia: Society
of Architectural Historians and The
Philadelphia Museum of Art, 1964.

Mellor, Meigs & Howe
A Monograph of the Works of Mellor, Meigs & Howe. New York: The Architectural Book Publishing Company, 1923.

O'Gorman, James F.; Thomas, George E.; and Myers, Hyman
Frank Furness, Architect. Philadelphia: Philadelphia Museum of Art, 1973.

Philadelphia City Planning Commission
A List of Notable Buildings in Philadelphia. Philadelphia: City Planning Commission, 1965.

Regional Planning Federation of the Philadelphia Tri-State District
The Regional Plan of the Philadelphia Tri-State District. Philadelphia: Regional Planning Federation of the Philadelphia Tri-State District, 1932.

Scharf, J. Thomas, and Westcott, Thompson
History of Philadelphia, 1609-1884. Philadelphia: L. H. Everts & Co., 1884.

Scully, Vincent, Jr.
Louis I. Kahn. New York: Braziller, 1962.

Stanton, Phoebe B.
The Gothic Revival and American Church Architecture, an Episode in Taste 1840-1856. Baltimore: The Johns Hopkins Press, 1968.

Strahan, Edward, ed. (pseud. for Earl Shinn)
A Century After, Picturesque Glimpses of Philadelphia and Pennsylvania. Philadelphia: Allen, Lane & Scott and J. W. Lauderbach, 1875.

Tatum, George B.
Penn's Great Town. Philadelphia: University of Pennsylvania Press, 1961.

Taylor, Frank H., ed.
The City of Philadelphia (in the Year 1900). Philadelphia: Trades League of Philadelphia, 1900.

Tinkcom, Harry M. and Margaret B.; Simon, Grant Miles
Historic Germantown. Philadelphia: American Philosophical Society, 1955.

Wainwright, Nicholas B.
Philadelphia in the Romantic Age of Lithography. Philadelphia: Historical Society of Pennsylvania, 1958.

Wallace, Philip B.
Colonial Houses, Pre-Revolutionary
Period, Philadelphia. New York: Architectural Book Publishing Company,
1931.

Warner, Sam Bass, Jr.
The Private City, Philadelphia in Three
Periods of Growth. Philadelphia: Uni-
versity of Pennsylvania Press, 1968.

Watson, John F.
Annals of Philadelphia and Pennsylvania.
Vol. I, 1830; Vol. II, 1850; Vol. III,
added 1877 by Willis P. Hazard; later
editions, Philadelphia: J. M. Stoddart & Co.

Westcott, Thompson
The Historic Mansions and Buildings of
Philadelphia. Philadelphia: Porter, 1877.

White, Theodore B., ed.
Philadelphia Architecture in the Nineteenth Century. Philadelphia: University of Pennsylvania Press, 1953.

Wurman, Richard S., and Feldman,
Eugene
The Notebooks and Drawings of Louis
I. Kahn. Philadelphia: Falcon Press,
1962.

Wurman, Richard S., and Gallery,
John A.
Man-Made Philadelphia. Cambridge:
MIT Press, 1972.

Young, John Russell
A Memorial History of the City of
Philadelphia from Its First Settlement
to the Year 1895. New York: N. Y.
History Company, 1895.

Articles and
Theses:

Ames, Kenneth
"Robert Mills and the Philadelphia Row
House." Journal of the Society of Architectural Historians, Vol. 27, May 1968,
pp. 140-146.

American Institute of Architects/
T-Square Club
Annual Exhibition Catalogues, 1894—
1931, 1949 to date.

Antiques
Vol. 82, November 1962 (entire issue
devoted to Fairmount Park and its
houses).

L'Architettura Cronache e Storia
Vol. 18, July 1972, pp. 72-129; memo-
rial to Oskar Stonorov including articles
by Bruno Zevi, Frederick Gutheim,
Edmund Bacon, and Otto Reichert-
Facilides.

Bacon, Edmund N.
"Downtown Philadelphia: A Lesson in
Design for Urban Renewal." Architectural Record, Vol. 129, May 1961,
pp. 131-146.

Baigell, Mathew E.
"John Haviland." Unpublished thesis,
University of Pennsylvania, 1965.

Baigell, Mathew E.
"John Haviland of Philadelphia."
Journal of the Society of Architectural Historians, Vol. 25, October 1966,
pp. 197-208.

Barefoot, N. Carl., Jr.
"The Philadelphia Story." American
Institute of Architects Journal, Vol.
35, June 1961, pp. 91-95.

Cooledge, Harold Norman, Jr.
"Samuel Sloan (1815-64), Architect."
Unpublished thesis, University of
Pennsylvania, 1963.

Cooledge, Harold Norman, Jr.
"Samuel Sloan and the Philadelphia
Plan." Journal of the Society of
Architectural Historians, Vol. 23,
October 1964, pp. 151-154.

Cram, Ralph Adams
"The Work of Frank Miles Day and
Bro." Architectural Record, Vol. 15,
May 1904, pp. 397-421.

Cram, Ralph Adams
"The Work of Messrs. Cope and
Stewardson." Architectural Record,
Vol. 16, October 1904, pp. 407-438.

Dallett, Francis James
"John Notman Architect." Princeton
University Library Chronicle, Vol. 20,
Spring 1959, pp. 127-139.

Eberlein, Harold Donaldson
"Pastorius Park, Philadelphia and Its
Residential Development." Architectural Record, Vol. 39, January 1916,
pp. 24-39.

Elliott, Huger
"Architecture in Philadelphia and a
Coming Change." Architectural Record,
Vol. 23, April 1908, pp. 294-309.

[Eyre, Wilson, no author]
"The Work of Wilson Eyre." Architectural Record, Vol. 14, October 1903,
pp. 280-325.

Fairbanks, Jonathan
"John Notman: Church Architect."
Unpublished thesis, University of
Delaware, 1961.

Fitz-Gibbon, Costen
"Architectural Philadelphia, Yesterday
and Today." Architectural Record,
Vol. 34, July 1913, pp. 20-45 (entire
issue devoted to Philadelphia architecture).

Githens, Alfred Morton
"Wilson Eyre and His Work." Architectural Annual, Vol. 2, 1900, pp 121-
184.

Jordy, William H.
"PSFS: Its Development and Its Significance in Modern Architecture."
Journal of the Society of Architectural
Historians, Vol. 21, May 1962, pp. 47-
83.

Maass, John
"Philadelphia City Hall, Monster or
Masterpiece." American Institute of
Architects Journal, Vol. 43, February
1965, pp. 23-30.

Massey, James C.
"Frank Furness in the 1800's."
Charette, Vol. 43, February 1963, n.p.

Massey, James C.
"Frank Furness in the 1880's"
Charette, Vol. 43, October 1963, pp.
25-29.

Massey, James C.
"Frank Furness, the Declining Years."
1890-1912." Charette, Vol. 46, February
1966, pp. 8-13.

Murtaugh, William
"The Philadelphia Row House." Journal
of the Society of Architectural Historians, Vol. 16, December 1957, pp. 8-13.

Nolan, Thomas
"Recent Suburban Architecture in Philadelphia and Vicinity." Architectural Record, Vol. 19, March 1906, pp. 167-193.

[Pennsylvania houses, no author]
"The Pennsylvania Type: A Logical Development, Recent Work by Mellor & Meigs, D. Knickerbocker Boyd and Duhring, Okie & Ziegler." Architectural Record, Vol. 32, March 1912, pp. 306-327.

Perspecta 9/10: The Yale Architectural Journal, 1965, articles by Romaldo Giurgola, Louis I. Kahn, and Robert Venturi.

Poppeliers, John C.
"The 1867 Philadelphia Masonic Temple Competition." Journal of the Society of Architectural Historians, December 1967, Vol. 26, pp. 279-284.

Reid, Kenneth
"Paul Philippe Cret, Master of Design." Pencil Points, October 1938, Vol. 19, pp. 607-638.

Roach, Hannah Benner
"The Planting of Philadelphia, A Seventeenth Century Real Estate Development." Pennsylvania Magazine of History, Part I, Vol. 92, January 1968, pp. 3-47; Part II, Vol. 92, April 1968, pp. 143-194.

Rowan, Jan C.
"Wanting To Be, The Philadelphia School." Progressive Architecture, Vol. 42, April 1961, pp. 130-163.

Stern, Richard A. M.
"PSFS: Beaux Arts Theory and Rational Expressionism." Journal of the Society of Architectural Historians, Vol. 21, May 1962, pp. 84-102.

Tinkcom, Margaret
"Southwark, a River Community: its Shape and Significance," Proceedings of the American Philosophical Society, Vol. 114, August 20, 1970, pp. 327-342.

[Trumbauer, Horace, no author]
"A New Influence in the Architecture of Philadelphia (The Work of Horace Trumbauer)." Architectural Record, Vol. 15, February 1904, pp. 93-121.

Van Trump, James D.
"The Gothic Fane: The Medieval
Vision and Some Philadelphia Churches,
1860-1900." Charette, Part I, Vol. 63,
September 1963, pp. 20-27; Part II,
Vol. 63, December 1963, pp. 14-21.
(Mr. Van Trump has done numerous
additional articles on Philadelphia
churches for the same publication.)

Webster, Richard J.
"Stephen D. Button." Unpublished
thesis, University of Delaware, 1963.

Weisman, Winston
"Philadelphia Functionalism and
Sullivan." Journal of the Society of
Architectural Historians, Vol. 20,
March 1961, pp. 3-19.

Wodehouse, Lawrence
"John McArthur, Jr. (1823-1890)."
Journal of the Society of Architectural
Historians, Vol. 28, December 1969,
pp. 271-283.

Zodiac 17
"USA Architecture, 1967."
Articles on and by Romaldo Giurgola,
Louis I. Kahn, Frank Schlesinger,
and Robert Venturi.

The Philadelphia Historical Commission
has accurately documented hundreds of
buildings within the city limits. Most of
their efforts have been focused on work
dating before the mid-nineteenth century. Data are filed by street address.
The files of the Historic American Buildings Survey in the Library of Congress
contain considerable information on
recently demolished structures in addition to important buildings still standing. The Campbell Scrapbooks and
many additional records in the Historical Society of Pennsylvania and the
scrapbooks and Seder files at the Free
Library of Philadelphia should also be
considered primary sources.

Index of Building Type and Style

Stores
85
Theaters
62, 63, 66, 89, 105, 163, 168
YWCAs
109

Note: With widely varying opinions regarding proper terminology for architectural styles, particularly in the late nineteenth and early twentieth centuries, only general categories are used here. Approximate inclusive dates given are based upon work covered in this book and are not necessarily reflective of the general dates for the periods cited.

Georgian Style (1700-1776)
30(CC I 1A), 34(CC I 9), 40, 41(CC I 20-24), 43(CC I 29), 46(CC II 1, CC II 3), 48(CC II 7-9), 49(CC II 11, CC II 13), 50(CC II 14A, B, D, F), 52(CC II 20), 53(CC II 22), 54(CC II 26), 60(CC III 11), 121(FP 8, FP 11), 122(FP, 12), 123(FP 17), 125(FP 22) 126(FP 25), 132(NP I 1), 149(NP II 4), 170(NE II 7), 171(NE II 12), 176(SP 1), 178(SP 3), 181(SP 13A, SP 15), 207(WP I 47), 210(WP II 3), 211(WP II 6), 212(WP II 8), 219(GM I 2B, GM I 3), 220(GM I 5), 221(GM I 8, GM I 10), 223(GM I 15-16), 224(GM I 17-20), 232(GM I 42), 233 (GM I 45), 234(GM I 48), 240(GM II 1)
Federal Style (1776-ca. 1840)
30(CC I 1B, C, CC I 2), 37(CC I 18), 42(CC I 25-26), 46(CC II 2), 47(CC II 5), 50(CC II 14E),52(CC II 19A, CC II 20), 53(CC II 23), 54(CC II 27-29), 55(CC II 31), 56(CC II 33, CC II 36), 57(CC III 37-38), 60(CC III 3), 61(CC III 5), 62(CC III 6, CC III 8), 63 (CC III 11),

64(CC III 12), 69(CC III 27), 95(CC VI 8), 120(FP 5), 121(FP 9-10), 122(FP 13), 123(FP 16), 125(FP 24), 126(FP 26), 150(NP II 7-8), 157(NP III 7), 165(NE I 12A), 168(NE II 2), 176(SP 1), 200(WP I 34), 204(WP I 40), 212(WP II 9), 218(GM I 1), 219(GM I 2A, C), 220(GM I 6), 224(GM I 19), 248(GM II 19)

Classical Revival (ca. 1800-ca. 1860)
32(CC I 7), 34(CC I 10), 35(CC I 14), 36(CC I 15, CC I 17), 38(CC I 19), 48(CC II 10), 53(CC II 24), 55(CC II 30), 57(CC II 39), 62(CC III 7), 63(CC III 10), 64(CC III 12), 65(CC III 14-16), 68(CC III 23), 72(CC IV 1), 89(CC V 28), 118(FP 1), 120(FP 6), 122(FP 13), 133(NP I 4), 134(NP I 6), 137-138(NP I 16), 139(NP I 18), 155-156(NP III 4), 170(NE II 9), 179(SP 6), 180(SP 9), 205(WP I 42)

Gothic Revival (ca. 1800-ca. 1860)
56(CC II 34), 73(CC IV 5), 92(CC VI 1), 119(FP 4), 139(NP I 17), 155(NP III 3), 169(NE II 6), 195(WP I 28), 207(WP I 48), 211(WP II 4), 225-227(GM I 21), 233(GM I 43)

Italianate Modes (ca. 1840-c. 1870)
33(CC I 8C, D, F), 34(CC I 11), 35(CC I 13), 36(CC I 16), 38(CC I 19), 43(CC I 28), 47(CC II 4), 52(CC II 19C), 55(CC II 32), 60(CC III 1), 61(CC III 4), 64(CC III 13), 72(CC IV 3), 77(CC IV 14), 80(CC V 3), 87(CC V 21), 89(CC V 27), 92(CC VI 2B), 93(CC VI C, D), 94(CC VI 6), 96(CC VI 11), 100(CC VI 24),

108(CC VII 1), 109(CC VII 5), 132(NP I 2), 134(NP I 7), 135(Np I 11), 137-138(NP I 16), 142-143(NP I 24) 162(NE I 1), 164(NE I 10), 168(NE II 3), 171(NE II 11), 196(WP I 32), 200-201(WP I 35), 211(WP II 5), 220(GM I 4A), 222(GM I 12, GM I 13), 225-227(GM I 21), 232(GM I 40)

Miscellaneous Romantic Revivals (ca. 1840-ca. 1860)
31(CC I 5), 76(CC IV 11), 134(NP I 5), 155-156(NP III 4)

Second Empire and Related
Mid-Century Classicism (ca. 1860-ca. 1880)
74(CC IV 6), 81(CC V 4), 88(CC V 24), 95(CC VI 8A), 96(CC VI 11), 111(CC VII 8), 125(FP 21), 137-138(NP I 16), 142-143(NP I 24), 162(NE I 2), 198(WP I 33C)

High Victorian Style (ca. 1865-ca. 1890)
33(CC I 8B), 38(CC I 19), 61(CC III 4), 68(CC III 23), 72(CC IV 2), 73(CC IV 5), 76(CC IV 10), 77(CC IV 15) 80(CC V 1), 83(CC V 8), 87(CC V 19), 89(CC V 28), 95(CC VI 9), 96(CC VI 11), 97(CC VI 13), 98(CC VI 17), 99(CC VI 19), 102-103(CC VI 27-31), 104(CC VI 33), 105(CC VI 34), 112(CC VII 13), 118-119(FP 2), 123(FP 14), 124(FP 18-19), 127(FP 27), 133(NP I 3), 137-138(NP I 16), 140(NP I 19, NP I 20A), 141(NP I 22), 142-144(NP I 24-27), 145(NP I 29), 156(NP III 4L), 157(NP III 6, NP III 7), 163(NE I 4), 165(NE I 12-14), 171(NE II 10), 177(SP 2),

178(SP 4), 179(SP 7), 180(SP 10, SP 12) 187(WP I 3), 190-191(WP I 13), 191(WP I 14), 194(WP I 22), 195(WP I 25, WP I 27, WP I 29), 197-202(WP I 33-36), 205(WP I 44), 220(GM I 4B, GM I 7), 222(GM I 14), 225-227(GM I 21), 228(GM I 22), 230(GM I 29), 231 (GM I 34), 237(GM I 55-56), 243(GM II 10-11), 250(GM II 24), 252(GM II 28)

Romanesque Revival (ca. 1880-ca. 1895)

68(CC III 22), 86(CC V 18), 109(CC VII 4), 141(NP I 21), 142-143(NP I 24)

Queen Anne Revival, Shingle Style, and Related Creative Eclecticism, (ca. 1880-ca. 1895)

66(CC III 17, CC III 18), 68(CC III 24), 69(CC III 25), 94(CC VI 4-5), 95(CC VI 8B), 97(CC VI 12), 98(CC VI 16), 104(CC VI 16), 104(CC VI 32), 105 (CC VI 36), 134(NP I 9), 137-138(NP I 16), 142-143(NP I 24), 144(NP I 28), 148(NP II 3), 165(NE I 12C), 206(WP I 46), 225-227(GM I 21), 228(GM I 24), 229(GM I 26, GM I 27), 236-237(GM I 52-54), 251(GM II 26-27)

Turn of the Century Eclecticism (ca. 1890-ca. 1930)

31(CC I 3, CC I 5), 32(CC I 6), 33(CC I 8A, E), 34(CC I 12), 42(CC I 27), 49 (CC II 12), 63(CC III 9), 69(CC III 26), 76(CC IV 12), 77(CC IV 15), 83(CC V 7, CC V 9), 84(CC V 10-11), 85-86(CC V 13-15), 88-89(CC V 23-26), 92(CC VI 1, CC VI 2A), 93(CC VI 3), 95-97(CC VI 10-12), 98(CC VI 15), 99(CC VI 18, CC VI 20), 100(CC VI 21, 22),101(CC VI 26), 105(CC Vi 35, CC VI 37), 108 (CC VII 2), 109-110(CC VII 6) 111 (CC VII 10), 112(CC VII 12), 113(CC VII 14), 119(FP 2K), 125(FP 22), 136(NP I 24A), 148(NP II 1), 156(NP III 4J, K), 163(NE I 4, NE I 5), 165(NE I 11), 178(SP 5), 181(SP 13B), 187(WP I 4), 188(WP I 9), 189(WP I 10), 191-192 (WP I 15-17), 195(WP I 26, WP I 30), 196(WP I 31), 200(WP I 35A), 205(WP I 43), 206(WP I 45), 210(WP II 1), 221 (GM I 9), 222(GM I 11), 225-227(GM I 21), 228(GM I 25), 229(GM I 28), 230(GM I 30), 233(GM I 44), 234 (GM I 46-47), 235(GM I 49-50), 236(GM I 52), 240-242(GM II 3-7), 244-246 (GM II 12), 248-249(GM II 18-23), 250(GM II 25), 252(GM II 29-30, GM II 32), 253(GM II 33)

Moderne Style (ca. 1925-c. 1940)

73(CC IV 4), 86(CC V 16), 87(CC V 20), 88(CC V 22), 100(CC VI 23), 113 (CC VII 15), 119(FP 3), 136(NP I 14), 149(NP II 5), 150(NP II 6), 151(NP II 9), 162(NE I 1), 163(NE I 7), 168(NE II 1), 181(SP 14), 186(WP I 1), 200(WP I 34), 231(GM I 33), 249(GM II 22)

International Style and Related Modern Architecture (ca. 1930-1960)

74(CC IV 7), 75(CC IV 8), 82-83(CC V 6), 85(CC V 12), 94(CC VI 7), 95 (CC VI 8C), 112(CC VII 11), 151(NP II 10), 154(NP III 1), 157(NP III 5),

164(NE I 9), 169(NE II 4, NE II 5), 186(WP I 2), 190(WP I 12), 204(WP I 41), 207(WP I 49), 211(WP II 7), 213 (WP II 10), 230(GM I 31), 231(GM I 35, GM I 36-38), 242(GM II 8), 247 (GM II 14), 252(GM II 31), 253(GM II 34)

Recent Modern Architecture (1960-Present)

31(CC I 4-5), 47(CC II 6), 50-51(CC II 15-18), 52(CC II 21), 54(CC II 25, CC II 27), 57(CC II 37), 60(CC III 2), 67 (CC III 19), 68(CC III 20), 76(CC IV 13), 77(CC IV 16), 80(CC V 2), 82(CC V 5-6), 84(CC V 10), 86(CC V 17), 88 (CC V 22), 97(CC VI 14), 101(CC VI 25), 105(CC VI 38), 108(CC VII 3), 110(CC VII 7), 111(CC VII 9), 120 (FP 7), 135(NP I 10), 140(NP I 20B), 141(NP I 23), 148(NP II 2), 163(NE I 8), 180(SP 11), 188(WP I 5-8), 189 (WP I 10), 190(WP I 11), 193-194(WP I 18-21, WP I 23-24), 195(WP I 26), 203(WP I 37-38), 210(WP II 1-2), 228 (GM I 23), 231(GM I 32), 232(GM I 39), 240(GM II 2), 246(GM II 13), 247(GM II 15-17)

Index of Buildings and Places

DATE DUE